DEDICATION

This book is dedicated to my beautiful bride, Cindy, and my three wonderful children: Hunter, Ciera, and Madi. Without your unfailing patience and encouragement, this book would have never happened. I love you all very much!

Thanks to Mom, Dad, and Tony. Your input, advice, and support have meant the world to me.

I can't forget all of my extended family and friends, whom have been great cheerleaders. There are too many of you to list! Special shout-outs to Justin Lee and Gino Santa Maria for all your help. You are both geniuses!

Most important, all glory and honor to my lord and savior, Jesus Christ! Words can't describe my appreciation and humility for your mercy and grace!

HOW TO GET ON THE . . .

CAREER FAST TRACK

A PROVEN, 5-STEP SYSTEM
FOR LANDING YOUR DREAM JOB,
FASTER THAN YOU EVER THOUGHT
POSSIBLE!

BRANDON GRIEVE

For information address:
Career Fast Track, LLC
1205 Woodcrest Lane
Hazelwood, MO 63042
www.mycareerfasttrack.com

First edition August 2012

Cover design and author photo by:
Gino Santa Maria at Santa Maria Studios
www.shutterfree.com

Copyediting by:
Katherine Pickett at POP Editorial Services
www.popediting.net
and
Michael Garrett at Creative Inspirations, Inc.
www.manuscriptcritique.com

For information about special discounts for bulk purchases, please contact Career Fast Track, LLC at (314) 830-3828 or info@mycareerfasttrack.com.

ISBN-10: 0985830506
ISBN-13: 978-0-9858305-0-2

CONTENTS

INTRODUCTION

Ugh, do I really have to go to work today? Have you ever had a case of "the Mondays," languishing in the thought of facing another week at a job you hate? Maybe you do not *hate* your job, but it leaves you feeling unfulfilled, that you are at a dead end in your career, or that what you do is of little or no significance. You just flat-out feel that it is time for a change . . . a radical change! Others may be saying, "I wish I had one of the problems above. I do not even have a job, let alone one I would like to change." If you were laid off, fired, down-sized, right-sized, had to quit for some reason, had a failed business—whatever the cause, you may be one of the millions of people in America and around the world who are unemployed.

Regardless of your reason, you feel that it is time

to start looking for a new job. Perhaps you have already started the process but are struggling with this overwhelming task. Either way, finding a job in this day and age can be challenging, especially if you are unprepared.

Let's face it, times are tough right now. Economic turmoil, increased government involvement, technological advancements, and changes in hiring practices have turned the job market on its head. Toss in the fact that people all over the world are increasingly unhappy with their jobs in general. Indeed, some industry surveys suggest that as many as 80 percent of all those interviewed are dissatisfied with their current job—a 20 percent increase from just twenty years ago. What we have is a perfect storm of conditions that has created a lot of competition for jobs, and not just the *good* jobs!

At this point, you are probably thinking, "Jeez, Mr. Sunshine, do you have any *good* news?" As a matter of fact, I do! Despite these challenges, there are plenty of opportunities for those who know the secrets of an effective job search and, more important, career planning. You see, some of the same conditions that have created more competition in the job market can also aid you in your job hunt. As daunting as the task of looking for a new job can seem, if you follow a proven, step-by-step process, you too can find not just any job, but the job of your dreams.

"Okay, Brandon; so what makes you the expert?" If you are thinking this right now, do not worry; I take no offense! I will offer, however, that I have faced about every circumstance I mentioned previously. I have hated jobs, felt like I was not living up to my potential, felt stuck, and was generally unhappy. I have also been fired and laid off from jobs and have been otherwise unemployed due to a failed business attempt. Trust me; I did not have a stellar early career track record. I struggled financially, to the point of near bankruptcy, and quite frankly, life was miserable!

With a wavering, yet undying, desire for success and fulfillment, and with a wife and children at home who tend to want to eat every now and then, I found the motivation to press on. Drawing from everything I had ever learned in my study of business and personal achievement, I devoted myself to the goal of finding the secret to career *bliss*. After practicing much patience and determination, I finally found a formula that led to what would be considered career success by most people's standards. I have personally used the principles and practices provided in this book to find jobs for myself and several others, so I know they work. I now want to share them with you!

More important, I sincerely want you to grasp this fact: *you* too can use this information to land *your* dream job. Before you raise an eyebrow, know that this is not rocket science. It only takes the right process, coupled with determination and a little elbow grease (yep, you have to *work* at it!), to make it happen for you. The determination and elbow grease are up to you; the process you can learn from this book. Just keep reading. I can assure you, if you diligently follow this five-step process with all the passion you can muster, you will get on the *Career Fast Track*!

So, why do I care about your career? When I was a young teenager, I had the pleasure of seeing one of my favorite motivational speakers at a live conference, the one and only Zig Ziglar! Now, I must admit, this was many years ago, so I do not remember everything he said that day, but I will never forget this one phrase:

You can have everything you want in life if you will just help enough other people get what they want. That's powerful!

Those words have stuck with me all these years, and I have tried to incorporate this principle into every aspect of my life. It has become a bit of a personal mantra. As such, nothing would make me happier than to know that I have contributed to your success in some way. It is my calling, my life's mission, and why you are reading these pages.

What makes this book different from other career books? First, this book is written from the perspective of a real worker who has learned what works and what does not, the hard way. It is not theory and not derived from academia. My background was not that of a career counselor or human resources professional. I personally learned the information I am about to share from the school of *hard knocks*, in the trenches, through trial and error. Second, you will find that this book is noticeably shorter than many other job search books on the market. This is not an indication that this book is lacking of substance or usable how-to information. The approach is just different.

I have intentionally left out a bunch of the *fluff* found in many other books. Right now, you need or want a job, not an intellectual history lesson, an exhaustive pep talk, or a lecture on how Maslow's Hierarchy of Needs relates to your job search. I want this information to be easily accessible so you can get down to business!

As you will soon come to see, I share information about things like how to write a resume, job search resources, interviewing tips, as well as many other topics. It was a conscious decision, however, not to go into painful detail about each of these areas. There are many books that provide these specific details, and I have no intention of reinventing the wheel.

My goal, rather, is to provide you with an easy-to-follow process to map out your destination. Where necessary, you can leverage other resources to fill in the gaps and gain additional information or details about the individual topics. I have created a resource page at the back of this book to get you started. You can also find suggestions at www.mycareerfasttrack.com.

You will also find exercises at the end of most of chapters to help you take action on the material presented. Taking action helps you learn and retain the material better, and it moves the information out of the theory realm and into the realm of practical, hands-on tools.

All that being said, let's preview what we will be discussing in the coming pages. There are essentially five steps that you must take, or high-level activities you must engage in, to complete the process of an effective career search and land that dream job:

1. Planning: getting in the right mental state and figuring out what the heck you want to do
2. Preparing: developing the tools, such as a resume and cover letter, necessary to aid you in your search
3. Searching: hitting the proverbial pavement and stirring up opportunities
4. Interviewing: getting in front of real employers and selling YOU
5. Negotiating: working with employers to settle on a mutually agreeable compensation package (my personal favorite)

Anyone who has ever had success obtaining a respectable career position has, in one form or another, gone through these stages. Unfortunately, the problem is that many do so without realizing it. Rather than being aware of the process and deliberately and methodically walking through it, they allow the process to happen to them. Call it fate, hope, or chance, sometimes they find a job. As it is said, "Even a blind squirrel occasionally finds a nut." Ask them how they did it, though, and ask them to repeat it if necessary. Often they are at a loss. Hope, though important, is not a strategy! It cannot be luck either. Luck is when opportunity meets preparation. We make our own luck!

So, are you ready to make some *luck* in your career? (Say yes.)

Great! Let's get *you* on the *Career Fast Track* . . .

1 WELCOME TO THE NEW WORLD

While many people feel like they are ready for a new job, or more important, a new career, most do not know where to begin the search. If you have not been in the job market in the past several years, things have certainly changed. As previously mentioned, jobs are scarcer than they were just a few short years ago, and there is a lot of competition for those jobs that remain. A *perfect storm* of conditions, spearheaded by a weak economy and advancements in technology, has not only made the job market tougher to succeed in, but also has drastically changed how we look for jobs.

The economic climate has been devastating to the labor market in the United States and around the world over the past few years. According to the US Bureau of Labor Statistics, the unemployment rate in the summer of 2012 was well over 8.0 percent, nearly double what it was just five years earlier. And it seems to only be getting worse. Just when the so-called financial *experts* say, "We are coming out of it," we receive more bad news about foreclosures, bankruptcies (business and personal), and unemployment rates, all of which are interrelated and collectively kill what little progress had been made previously. One look at your retirement account statements is all the proof you need!

This financial meltdown has stricken fear in the minds of companies who would otherwise be hiring. Even many of those businesses that have managed to survive and thrive have slowed down or completely stopped hiring altogether. FUD—fear, uncertainty, and doubt—has caused these organizations to carefully guard their capital reserves and cash flow just as a momma bird protects her fragile eggs. Many companies are even preemptively downsizing, not because of poor earnings but rather out of anticipation of tougher times. Everyone seems to be on the defensive, in survival mode.

Even the popular, and still relatively hot, field of information technology (IT), where I come from, is taking a hit. Not long ago, I ran into a former six-figure income earner who had been laid off from his job and was selling shoes in a retail store to get by. Not that there is anything wrong with selling shoes, or even working in retail, for that matter; but the point is, this individual was in a position where he had to take a job doing something he did not enjoy for less than half of what he previously earned. Tragic!

There have been many other changes in the field of job search in the past several years. Some of the more traditional techniques of finding a job just aren't as effective as they used to be. The surge of technology in our culture has forever changed the way job seekers look for work. There is no doubt that the method by which I found my last job is entirely different from the way I found my first. For instance, whereas the newspaper was once the go-to source for job postings, by today's standards, it is not the most efficient search technique, and many higher-paid career positions are not even posted there anymore. This does not mean the newspaper is an altogether bad tool to use, as we will discuss later, but it is not in the place of prominence it once held.

The market for job placement firms, recruiters,

staff augmentation, and consulting services has also exploded over the past decade. This is especially relevant for high-tech and professional fields such as information technology and health care, but it is becoming more prevalent in other industries as well. In fact, I have personally interviewed for positions that were not even advertised to the public by the employer. Some organizations choose to utilize the services of recruiting firms exclusively as a way to outsource the hassle of candidate screening.

If it is not glaringly obvious by now, a new approach is needed to be successful in the job search game these days. The tried-and-true methods of yesteryear just do not cut it anymore. Folks today have to be much savvier. You need to be organized and strategic in your approach. Throwing caution to the wind is a recipe for failure!

There are only so many jobs out there to be had, so who wins and who loses? The winners are those who take the time to step back and look at the bigger picture. Winners know that there is much more to career happiness than simply hopping on a job postings website, uploading a resume, and hoping for the best. Remember, hope is not a strategy!

The successful ones prepare themselves by carefully crafting a plan, like a labor of love. If you want to be in the winners' circle, you will need to have clearly defined goals, professional tools, an effective search process, tight interviewing skills, and solid negotiating tactics, not to mention a strong work ethic and some creativity. That is what I am here to help you with: laying out a plan and developing the skills that will allow you to beat the odds!

Now, if you would rather be on the losing side of the equation, ignore the previous paragraph. Some people lose because they are not willing to step up their game and go the extra mile. They do not want to put any *real* effort into the process.

"That's too hard; it takes too long. I've never had to work this hard at it before," they say.

Some are content to languish in mediocrity, letting the *good* jobs go to those who actually work for them. Some lose because they are irresponsible. They would rather sit idly by, waiting for handouts.

"Why not?" they may think. "Bailouts seem to be readily available these days!"

But, more commonly, the losers are simply those who fail to plan, fail to learn, and above all, fail to take the *right* action! Perhaps not because they are lazy or irresponsible; they just don't know how.

I know all this because I have been on the losing end. Early in my career, I was anything but lazy, and I was pretty mature for my age. I had the desire and work ethic to climb the corporate ladder and have a successful career; I just didn't know how. It is sad to say, but as a general rule, our public school system, and even most higher-education institutions, deserve a big, fat F when it comes to adequately preparing our young people for their careers ahead. Would-be workers attempt to enter the workforce ignorant and unprepared. They are too often left with mounds of student loan debt and no way of paying for it.

For me, ignorance was *not* bliss! I bounced around from job to job, trying to find something I was good at, something I was passionate about, and something that would provide a great income. I left nothing on the table—telemarketer, windows and siding salesperson, oil change technician, computer software trainer, sales manager, mortgage broker—all in only a half dozen years! I just could not find my niche. It's not that I did not want to settle down into a stable career, but the answers eluded me.

How did I finally find the key to my career success? First, I have to admit, there was not one silver bullet, no specific *aha* moment that immediately turned my world upside down. For me, learning slowly over time, a lot of research, asking for advice, modeling success, and trying new techniques, led to a system that I have been able to successfully leverage in recent years to achieve fantastic results.

The good news for you is that you do not have to spend years trying to figure it out on your own. I will share my story and process with you so that you, too, can find career success, faster than you imagined. So, are you going to be a winner or a loser? The decision is yours.

2 INSIDE LOOK AT THE JOURNEY

As I reflect back now, it is hard to imagine where I was just a little over a decade ago and how far I have come. If someone had told me back then that all my struggles were actually a blessing in disguise and that someday a greater good would come from it all, I would have . . . I don't know–laughed, cried, or punched them in the face–something like that! Have you ever done that? Have you gone through struggles that at the time seemed so hopeless and you felt you were doomed, only to look back years later and say, "I made it through, and now I am a better person for it"? As it is said, *what doesn't kill you makes you stronger!*

Yep, that's where I was once, in the depths of despair. Imagine looking in the mirror in your early twenties and doing an assessment of your life that went something like this:

Let's see . . . Wife? Check, got one!

Kid? Yep, got one of those too, and one on the way, because I am an overachiever!

Mortgage payment? Of course; the biggest one I could qualify for!

Mounds of debt? That is the American way, right?

Car? Ah, yes, an old beater that doesn't run right half the time!

And for good measure, let's top it off with . . . NO JOB!

Holy crap, what have I gotten myself into? How did I get to this place? This isn't what I expected out of life!

The truth is, I *really* did not expect to be at that place in my life . . . ever! Who does? The surprising and disappointing part of it was that I had always expected that I would do something great, *be* someone great. As a teenager, I would listen to my parents' self-help, motivational tape programs (yes, they were cassette tapes back then). I am talking about some of the great inspirational leaders of our time: Zig Ziglar,

Brian Tracy, Tony Robbins, Jim Rohn, and others. I even attended several live seminars with some of these personal heroes. I learned a lot, and looking back, I was motivated and wise beyond my years. I do not mean to pat myself on the back, but honestly, how many high school kids do you know who would give up their free time to study the lessons of self-help gurus?

I was determined. I was going to be the next *golden boy*—motivational speaker, corporate bigwig, professional musician. So, why didn't I? What happened in those few short years after high school?

Let's flash back to my little moment of self-realization; you know, that *holy crap* moment. Truth be told, this was not an isolated event. There were many occasions just like this, when the reality of my situation set in. Sometimes with tears, sometimes with clenched fists, sometimes with fear and trembling, but each time, I questioned where I came from and where I was going. I was desperate for answers.

I mean, I was planning on going places, right? Ah, *places,* plural. One day it hit me. I started thinking about all these fantasies I had when I was younger. I also realized that they had something in common with all the careers I had attempted to no avail. There was no focus in my life. I did not have my eye on a single target, nor did I have a plan on how to get anywhere, let alone several *anywheres*. All that so-called motivation I once had was no more than youthful enthusiasm. Excitement, but no substance.

I finally realized that I had to put all that self-help knowledge to work. It was no longer just about dreaming big, positive thinking, or high energy; at some point the rubber had to meet the road. I had to focus, put a stake in the ground. Over a series of sessions, I sat down with pen and paper and started making lists. I took inventory of things I liked and didn't like about the various jobs I had held, interests, strengths, and weaknesses. I also set some real goals.

I had learned the hard way, though, that just setting nebulous *goals* would not get me to where I wanted to go. Both long-term goals (strategy) and short-term goals (tactics) would be required. After poring over my lists, I had come to some conclusions, but this also led me to many more questions. So, I patiently conducted research and interviewed industry experts over several months. It paid off; my questions were answered, and I made my decision. I had decided that I wanted to tackle the world of information technology. Specifically, I wanted to be on the engineering side of the business . . . a propeller head . . . a geek.

Great, I knew what my long-term goal was, but one does not just decide to be an IT expert (or any kind of expert), and—voilà—become one overnight. I needed a plan of action to obtain the knowledge and experience necessary to qualify me for that role. It was a big leap to go from salesperson to systems engineer. Step one was to get some training, so I enrolled in some classes at a local trade school. Fortunately, this came fairly easily for me, because I had some computer experience and loved technology.

I still had to earn a living while attending classes and earning industry certifications over the next couple of years, so I worked in a sales capacity for some local IT companies. Admittedly, I was not the best salesman in the world, but I got to be around the industry, learning from the pros and meeting contacts. Then, one day I got my first shot. A real gem of a human being, a great man and someone I consider a friend to this day, called me. We'll just call him Marty. He was expanding his IT consulting business and needed an extra hand. I had worked with him at a previous employer, and we hit it off. Marty had the confidence in me to give me a chance.

I thank God for Marty, along with his right-hand man, Allen, who together were phenomenal mentors and friends. Yes, I necessarily took a pay cut initially, as I was starting from the bottom of a new career field, but this was a calculated and strategic career move that has paid dividends many times over. While I have several years since moved on from that position, it was the start of what has become a fun and lucrative career.

As my career has progressed since that time, I have continued to hone my skills and solidify the process I use to manage my career and search for jobs. When it is time to make a change, which happens more often in IT than many other industries, I am better prepared and have the confidence necessary to make the right moves, each time progressing forward in my career. It is not easy, and it can be a time-consuming process, but then when do good things ever come easy? Winners make the tough choices, and losers complain, never going anywhere.

Though I still feel that I am a journeyman, I am blessed to have acquired some great knowledge and skills along the way that can help others. I did not set out to be an expert in the field of career planning, but as friends and family witnessed what I had accomplished, they started asking questions. They wanted to know what I did and how they could do the same. Some wanted help writing or reviewing their resumes. Some asked how to find job leads. Others wanted to know how to prepare for an interview, and still others wanted tips for negotiating a compensation package. Once I caught on to what was happening, I realized that I had been unknowingly achieving one of my greatest desires—helping others!

It is humbling to have so many people respect and trust my advice when it comes to their livelihoods. It has grown over the past few years; not by design, at least initially, but still it has happened. I feel blessed and believe that my experience is a gift from above, a gift that does not diminish when you give it away. Rather, it grows and propagates as it is shared. That is what excites me: knowing that I can have a positive influence on others and play some small part in their success.

So, am I unique? Are those I have mentored unique, or can this Career Fast Track model really work for others as well? I am here to tell you that it can and will work for you, if you devote yourself to the process. I am in no way special nor unique. I have not invented these concepts, nor have I discovered some secret unknown to mankind. I just happened to take what I have learned through the years and formalized the knowledge into a repeatable process that really works. I have personally helped coach others and have witnessed their success as they make their own way. This is now my life's journey: to continually learn so I am always equipped to help others help themselves. That is my new Career Fast Track!

3 THE SOLUTION . . . AT A GLANCE

So far, we have briefly defined the challenge that so many of us have faced, or are currently facing, with regard to our careers and our relative dissatisfaction with these careers. We also took a quick peek into the current state of the job market and what separates the winners from the losers, that is, those who are successful and those who are not. Finally, I gave you an inside look at my personal career struggles and how I overcame these struggles to achieve career success. In this chapter, I will provide a high-level overview of the process, an in-a-nutshell synopsis, if you will. The goal here is to allow you to see the bigger picture before we dive into the weeds, like looking at the picture on a puzzle box before assembling the pieces.

Essentially, there are five main practice areas you will need to master to maximize your chances of success when making a career change. These are the key milestones for the entire job search process, and they are the steps we will discuss in more detail throughout this book. This is the *Career Fast Track* model:

1. Planning
2. Preparing
3. Searching
4. Interviewing
5. Negotiating

Let's define each of these for clarity.

Planning. This almost sounds like a no-brainer, but it is the step most often overlooked. Skipping this step is the surest path to failure. Planning entails several smaller substeps that collectively form the foundation for the rest of the process. In fact, these disciplines are applicable to several areas of life and are the most critical in solving the aforementioned career woes. They include things like taking a step back and assessing what you like and dislike about your current and past jobs, taking an inventory of your skills and shortcomings, setting short- and long-term goals, and developing an action plan. It is a time for soul-searching, if you will. This is the fuel that powers the career engine!

Preparing. Once we have a solid grasp on our experience, skills, and objectives, we have to be able to articulate this in a manner easily digestible by potential employers. This includes creating a resume and cover letter—the practical tools of the trade that allow us to market ourselves to others. The resume and cover letter are analogous to pamphlets you receive in the mail from companies that are touting their products and services and trying to get your attention. Your job in this step is to create high-impact tools that cause you to stand out from the crowd. There is a bit of both art and science to this.

Searching. As its name implies, searching is the process of hitting the proverbial streets and looking for actual job opportunities. This involves leveraging every outlet possible, including professional and personal networks of contacts, recruiters, online job sites, social media, and other more traditional methods. With all these tools at our disposal, finding and applying for job openings is more efficient than ever before. However, like anything else, you cannot just run out there all *willy-nilly* and hope for the best; you must have an effective strategy. Failure to do so can be counterproductive and actually hurt you if you are not careful.

Interviewing. Come on, do I really have to explain what an interview is? If you have ever had a job in your life, you have been on an interview. Maybe formal, maybe informal, perhaps in person or on the phone; regardless of what form it took, you spoke with a potential employer about a job before he or she decided to hire you and you decided to take the job. Most people understand, of course, that an interview is the employer's opportunity to screen potential candidates to determine if they would be a good fit for the company, but this is only half the story. What most job seekers do not realize is that an interview is *our* chance to vet the employers as well. If your idea of an interview is a one-sided exchange where you sit and sweat through a barrage of questions, hoping to survive the onslaught, think again.

Negotiating. This is my favorite part of the job search process. I absolutely love it! Here's the scenario: You have proceeded through the often tedious process of applying for a position, attended several phone and/or face-to-face interviews, submitted references, perhaps completed a personality profile, etc., etc. Then a hiring manager or human resources (HR) representative approaches you to let you know that you are the chosen candidate and that the company would like to extend you a job offer. So, if they want you, and you want the job, you accept the offer, right? *Wrong!* This is the moment where you have the most leverage you will likely ever have to demand what you feel you are worth. Use it wisely!

And that's it. That's how you land a job. With such easy steps to follow, what could possibly go wrong? It can't be that difficult, right? I mean, this is first-grade stuff. Piece of cake!

Paradoxically, this assumption in and of itself is one of several reasons job seekers often derail in the process. They underestimate what it really takes. The truth is, finding a job is, or should be, so much more than just finding a job.

The process of finding a job should merely be a tactical step in a larger, more strategic plan. What we are really talking about here is career management. It is not that it is a terribly difficult concept, but you have to be diligent. As we have already discussed, jobs are not as easy to come by as they used to be, and there is a lot more competition for those jobs. If you take it for granted, you will be left in the dust wondering what happened.

The remedy to this pitfall is simply to take the process seriously. After all, we are talking about your livelihood. There is nothing more serious than looking at an empty dinner plate, and that is exactly what is at stake here. Been there, done that! Do not assume that you can coast through a job search without giving it its due respect. Be prepared and give it your all.

If you are currently unemployed, make it your job to find a job. Approach the process as you would any other job. Wake up each morning and get yourself ready. Block out uninterrupted time during the day when you can stay focused. Realizing that you will gain in equal proportions to the effort you exert is the key to avoiding apathy!

Another large contributor to failure is skipping steps. You simply cannot take shortcuts and expect to achieve career success. Remember, I have been there. I learned the hard way that without all the components working in tandem, the whole thing collapses. The *Career Fast Track* is a holistic process, and the whole is greater than the sum of the parts.

You cannot afford to do only those things that come easily or conveniently and neglect the rest. To use an analogy, consider what would happen if train track builders failed to install those sections that required crossing a tough terrain, such as a mountain or river. The train wouldn't be able to complete its journey, would it? If you want to reach your destination of career success, you have to persist, even when the going gets tough.

The cause of this generally boils down to impatience, apathy, or both. As it is said, good things come to those who wait, and *no*, we are not talking about procrastination here. Make steady progress, but do so patiently and methodically. It is worth it!

Skipping steps and taking shortcuts may seem like a way to speed up the process, and it will; it is the quickest way to disqualify yourself from potential opportunities and ensure failure. Following the whole process without wavering is the shortest path to success! Be the tortoise, not the hare. Stick with it, and ask for help if you get stuck.

Fear is another major cause of failure. In fact, fear of failure itself is often a self-fulfilling prophecy. It is also common for many job seekers to be scared to death when going into interviews or negotiations. They often freeze under pressure due to a feeling of inadequacy or fear of rejection. Fear is a self-sabotaging emotion and is generally based on thoughts that are completely irrational.

Do you want to know a little secret? The managers and human resources professionals who are interviewing or negotiating with you are human beings too. They get nervous just like you do. They have something to lose also . . . *you*!

Employers have to compete with each other to recruit the best talent in the labor market. They know it is not easy to find qualified, high-caliber employees, and the thought of losing a quality candidate scares them. There is no need to fear. Always remember, you only fail if you fail to try. If you stumble, you can always get right back up. Embrace the opportunity to learn and focus on the desired outcome. Let success be your motivator and fear will melt away.

The final reason we will discuss as to why many job seekers fail is a *lone ranger* mentality. They try to do everything themselves. I am not suggesting that we should delegate or outsource ownership of our careers to others. I am simply saying that leveraging the assistance of others where possible provides a greater chance of success.

Others who have gone before you may have expertise in areas where you are not as strong. You can learn from them so as not to repeat their mistakes. You can also reach out to your network of contacts that can provide valuable job leads or personally introduce you to potential employers. The bottom line: Do not go it alone. Use every advantage you have!

Now that you know what to expect, we will spend the balance of the book diving into more detail about the Career Fast Track process and the individual steps. Each and every step will be addressed more clearly so that there is no guesswork involved. I want to help provide you the best chance to succeed. So, do not hesitate. Get ready, and let's go!

Step 1
Planning

Developing a Career Road Map

4 DO YOU *REALLY* NEED A NEW JOB?

The first step in the *Career Fast Track* process is planning. Breaking it down further, this involves taking a step back and doing a little soul-searching. For our purposes here, this means determining if making a career change is the right answer for you.

Every day, millions of unsatisfied workers wish that they could work for another company or even become self-employed. Is this you? While many think they have to switch jobs to be happy, not everyone actually needs to. That is why it is important to consider whether switching jobs is really in your best interest. In this chapter we will look at common reasons for and against making a change.

Reasons to Consider Quitting Your Job

Do you find yourself regularly working excessive, unwanted overtime, particularly where you have no choice in the matter? If so, this may be a sign that it is time to consider looking for a new job. Although some overtime here and there is okay, as it can be considered a part of the job, you should not be expected, nor forced, to work more overtime than you are comfortable with.

It is also important to consider overtime pay. Do you receive time and a half or other compensation for your overtime hours? If you are in a salaried position, you may be taken advantage of. If you are putting in tons of hours and are not being adequately compensated for those hours, a new job may be in your best interest. After all, you need some downtime to refresh and have fun. Life is too short!

Another reason you may want to consider searching for a new job is if you find it difficult to get time off from work. Of course, when examining time off, it is important that you do not take advantage of the situation. It is not acceptable to regularly request time off from work simply because you don't feel like working.

With that in mind, if you need to take time off for medical illnesses or family emergencies, you should be granted that time off. Work is important, but you should not be asked to compromise your health or that of your family for it. If you are being asked to do so, you may want to consider finding a new job.

A lack of advancement opportunity is another reason to start thinking about finding a new job. If you are interested in climbing the corporate ladder but your company does not make these opportunities available to its employees, you may want to consider seeking employment elsewhere. The same may be said in circumstances where promotion opportunities exist but you have been consistently passed over with no clear explanation.

Unfortunately, there are just some situations where you can work as hard as possible and never receive praise for your hard work, get a pay raise, nor see a promotion. This can be due to corporate politics and other factors, but whatever the reason, try to avoid, or remove yourself from, these types of situations at all costs. Long-term career success is largely dependent upon your ability to grow and be stretched with new challenges.

If you are not making enough money to support yourself or your family, this is usually a big motivator to look for a new job. That being said, if your primary motivation for considering alternate employment is to make more money, you may want to first consider speaking with your supervisors. It would not do any harm to ask for a pay raise, especially if you are already considering leaving the company. If you are able to see an increase in pay, you may want to consider staying at your current job.

In keeping with money, you will also want to examine the commute that you must make to and from your current job. If you have a long, expensive commute, it may be in your best interest to search for a new job that is closer to home or provides ample compensation to cover the daily trek. Unfortunately, when accepting a new job, many individuals do not consider the commute to and from work. If you are not careful, you may find yourself spending a large percentage of your time on the road and a large percentage of your income on fuel. At nearly $4 per gallon, this can add up quickly. Also, think about how much of your life a long, daily round-trip can consume. Quality of life is a *huge* factor and should not be overlooked.

The final consideration for switching jobs we will discuss is this: if you absolutely despise the work you do and feel like you just cannot take another day, it is time to get out. Life is too short to spend it doing something you hate. This kind of attitude will also have a large impact on the quality of your work and relationships with others. Without the right attitude, you will not perform as effectively as you could otherwise. This is not fair to your employer and can ultimately affect your own confidence.

Virtually every one of us was created with ample capabilities and the ability to choose what we do in life. It has been said that once you find what you love to do, you will never work another day in your life. I am not sure that I would 100 percent agree with this, as there will always be some aspects of our jobs that we are not crazy about. This is also true (if not especially true) for those who are self-employed. Nevertheless, this saying has some merit. It makes it more tolerable to get up in the morning if you know you will be doing something you enjoy.

These are just some of the most common situations you may encounter when deciding whether it is time to start seeking new employment opportunities. To be honest, though, you do not need a reason to quit your job. You are free to do what you want; it's your life! You have to live with the consequences, good or bad.

With that in mind, should you wish to change jobs, use your best judgment. This involves not quitting on impulse or without a solid plan in place. It is always better to take a step back and consider the ramifications of your actions.

Reasons *Not* to Quit Your Job

Regardless of your reason, whether it is that you dislike your boss, your coworkers, your work hours, the pay, or anything else about your job, the decision to quit is yours to make. Before you take the plunge, though, here is some food for thought. There are some instances in which you may want to reconsider your decision.

This sounds weird coming from a guy writing a book about how to find a new job, huh? Remember, my goal is to help you find happiness, whether that means you stay at your current job or find a new one. With that, a few instances where you may want to stay put at your current job are outlined here.

If you are disgruntled because you have a new boss and feel it's time to scram, you may want to rethink your decision. I have known several people who quit their jobs, or threatened to do so, because they did not get along with their new boss. If you have a new supervisor, you are encouraged to give it time. Many new supervisors are difficult at first, because they feel that they need to be, as though they have something to prove. Over time, however, you will find that most new managers will lighten up and let a new side of themselves show, possibly a more pleasant and friendlier side.

I have worked for managers whom I did not care for at first, but ended up liking down the road. It just takes time to get to know someone, his or her unique style, and how to effectively communicate with that person. If you were happy with your job before your new boss arrived, try giving it a few months before you decide to move on. You may be glad you did!

Are you annoyed by a coworker, particularly one who is located physically close to you at the office? While frustrating, this is another situation in which you may want to reconsider quitting job over. You should never give someone the power to make you want to quit your job, especially if it is just because you do not like that person.

Of course, you are advised to take your safety into consideration. If one of your coworkers is displaying behavior that may cause you harm, or provides a hostile work environment, you should take action right away. This action may ultimately include resigning from your job, but you should first consider contacting a supervisor or your company's human resources department. You should never have to quit your job because someone else is in the wrong.

A poor performance review is another situation in which you may not want to quit your job. Although it may seem embarrassing and frustrating if you ever receive a bad review, it is important to remember that it can happen to the best of people and the hardest of workers. No one can perform to perfect standards all of the time, and this is something you need to remember. Instead of quitting your job because of a poor review, leverage the review process as an opportunity to better yourself. You can set a goal of improving your work performance, which should result in a better review the next time around.

Were you passed by for a promotion? If so, and you feel that the only recourse is to quit your job, this may be a hasty action. This may seem contradictory to my comments in the previous section, but not necessarily so. Allow me to explain.

There are a number of different factors to consider when it comes to promotions and why you may have been passed up for one. Do you know why you were passed over? Was there another employee more qualified or who had more seniority than you? You can also use this situation as a way to improve your work skills by setting goals for yourself. With that in mind, if you regularly find yourself being passed up for promotions that you are more than qualified for, you may want to consider seeking employment elsewhere.

Simple boredom may also be an inadequate reason to quit your job. If you have a job that provides no challenge for you, it is easy to get in a rut. I would be lying if I told you that I have never quit a job for this reason, but if I had it to do all over again, I might reconsider.

Before you quit for such a reason, consider the options at your current employer first. You could start by looking at the job openings your company has available. Perhaps you would be well suited for, and may rather enjoy, another position internally.

Try this: Set up a one-on-one, face-to-face meeting with your supervisor. Explain to her that, while you enjoy working at the company and appreciate the job you have, you feel you are ready for some additional responsibilities that provide new challenges. If nothing else, your boss will appreciate the fact that you were bold enough to approach her and should recognize your drive. Those in management positions remember these things when it comes time for promotions, bonuses, and raises.

Again, these are just a handful of common situations where you may want to refrain from quitting your job, especially without careful consideration. Of course, there are extenuating circumstances to the situations mentioned here, such as ones that may involve sexual harassment or other dangerous situations in your workplace, but the point is not to be too hasty to jump ship.

If, after long and careful consideration, you have decided it is time for you to start looking for a new job, there are several things you should do in preparation. If you currently have a job, it is usually best to take these steps before you quit. Trust me; I speak from experience.

There is nothing worse than the pressure of wondering how you are going to pay the bills or where your next meal is coming from, particularly during a job search. Not only does this affect your confidence and focus, which is crucial, but it also puts you at a disadvantage. How so, you ask? Well, if it is not obvious by your resume, you will almost definitely be asked during an interview if you are currently employed. Once a potential employer knows you are not, a couple of things will surely happen:

1. Concerns will creep into their minds about why you are *really* unemployed and how reliable you would be as an employee.

2. You will lose much of your leverage when negotiating your compensation package (i.e., salary, benefits). Hiring managers, and those in human resources (HR) positions, are often experienced negotiators and will know you are desperate for some income. They will often

take advantage of this by "low-balling" their offer.

In closing this chapter, it is worth repeating how important it is to carefully consider your options and choices before acting on them. Impulse decisions are often a sign of emotional immaturity. I will say it again: if at all possible, keep your current job while you do the necessary preparation for your new job. It will definitely pay off in the form of peace of mind and, often, your future income.

I would also recommend that you talk to someone you trust and get outside, unbiased advice. It is also beneficial if this person has been through this situation before or has industry-specific expertise. People who do not have a "dog in the hunt," so to speak, can often provide a perspective that you are blind to.

Chapter 4 Exercises

Chapter 4 explored some of the scenarios where it may and may not be appropriate to consider looking for a new job. Now it is time to take action. The exercises in this section are designed to help you engage in serious thought about your own situation and to express those thoughts on paper.

The objectives of these exercises are twofold. First, they will help bring clarity, and hopefully good judgment, to your decision-making process. Second, they will help you identify those positive things about your current job that you want to ensure are present in your new job and the negative aspects you want to avoid. Your "likes" and "dislikes" should be considered when evaluating new career opportunities and should influence your decisions.

Please take the time to complete each exercise. Write the answers in a separate journal that you can refer back to and reflect upon.

1. List all the things you dislike about your current job. What frustrates you? What would you change if you could? Is it a dreadful boss, long hours, poor pay or benefits, etc.? There is no limit here. Now is the time to lay it all on the line, so be thorough and be honest with yourself.

2. Let's expand upon Exercise 1. Why do you dislike these particular things about your job? Address each item in your list individually and write down how these things make you feel. What need in your life is not being met due to these conditions? The goal here is to get to the heart, the psychology, of your answers in Exercise 1.

3. What do you like about your current job? Do you have a supportive boss, great pay or benefits, time off when you need it, or exciting and challenging work? Again, think about every

little detail, even something as seemingly insignificant as free parking. There are some cities where workers have to pay hundreds of dollars per month to park just to go to work.

4. As you did for the "dislikes," now let's address your "likes" more deeply. Again, approach each item individually. Why do you like these particular things about your job? When you think about these things, how do they make you feel? How do they benefit you?

5. Now, referring back to your list of "dislikes," what would have to change to turn these "dislikes" into "likes"? Is there anything within your power that you could do to change them? Are you *really* sure about that? Do you have the ear of someone who *does* have influence over such changes?

6. Compare your "likes" and "dislikes" lists. Which list has more items on it? Do the "likes" outnumber the "dislikes" or vice versa?

7. Even if the "likes" outnumber the "dislikes" in Exercise 6, are there any deal-breakers on the "dislikes" list? These are things that, alone, are critical enough to outweigh all the "likes" combined. If there are such items and you do not have the ability to directly change them nor influence the needed change, this is probably a sign that it is time to prepare for your departure.

5 SETTING CLEAR GOALS

Okay, you have decided that it is time to start the job search, so where do you go from here? Before you write your resume, start scanning the job search websites, or planning for interviews, all of which we will get to in due time, you need to set some goals. PLEASE DO NOT SKIP THIS STEP!

If you have never *really* set goals using a proven system, you cannot begin to understand the power that goals can have on your career, or any aspect of your life. Chances are, you have had some wishes, dreams, or desires in your life and worked toward them. How else have you accomplished anything? You must *have* a target before you can hit one.

While this is not a book about goal setting, per se, this should be an integral part of your career. In fact, you should integrate goal setting into all aspects of your life. As such, I have purposefully presented this section in a general way so you can apply the principles anywhere they are appropriate for you.

To achieve a goal, there is a specific system you should implement, which is sure to help your job search be more productive and rewarding. This process should be used to streamline and analyze your goals. A goal determines what action or plan is to be taken and defines the expected results. This plan provides a set of directions so that you can make decisions with clarity and purpose.

Peter Drucker wrote a book published in 1954 entitled *The Practice of Management* wherein the concept of MBO, or management by objectives, was introduced. *Objectives* is just another word for specific goals, and for our purposes here, they are used interchangeably. This is a program that consists of simple, but useful, processes to meet commitments in an organizational environment. But don't worry; this is also applicable to personal goals and plans.

The MBO concept was expanded on in 1981 by George T. Doran, who outlined a five-step, goal-setting formula. Goals should be:

1. **Specific.** Be as detailed as possible. For instance, instead of saying, "I want a new job," say, "I want to be a sales representative for a Fortune 500 multinational information technology company." In the latter statement, a specific role, industry, and company size was explicitly defined. Also, it is best to establish a single desired outcome per goal, rather than dividing your focus. A single objective cannot be derived if there are two or more results expected.

   What is important is that there is a need to clarify what is to be achieved, and it should have your full attention. If you desire multiple outcomes, set multiple complementary goals so that each can be tracked independently. This is near and dear to my heart, because lack of a specific, long-term goal is what caused much of my early career angst.

2. **Measurable.** Most things that are intangible are hard to measure, while others are easily measurable for the mere fact that they include numbers or ratings. Take service crews, for

example. It is hard to measure how the service was delivered, but if the number of complaints is counted, then there is a specific number that can be used to rate the effectiveness of the service.

Relating this specifically to job hunting, you may set a goal to schedule three interviews per week. The number of interviews is the specific metric by which to track your success. Furthermore, you will begin to understand how many jobs you have to apply for, on average, to accomplish that goal. If you are consistently falling short of your goal, you may have to adjust your tactics and try something different. Perhaps there is a problem with your resume or cover letter that a few minor tweaks could solve.

3. **Attainable.** Readily available resources provide information on if and how an objective can be attained. This must be derived from fact and be realistic. It could be that a certain goal is indeed realistic, but the time frame to reap the result may not be.

Also, it is better to state objectives based on facts. This promotes motivation, as opposed to an objective taken from unsubstantiated beliefs or feelings, as this may cause unexpected failure and a feeling of discouragement. For example, if you are just starting your career, it is not realistic to expect to be the CEO of a Fortune 500 company within one year. A more realistic one-year goal may be to become a team leader or department supervisor. Do your homework and know what is feasible, but allow yourself to be stretched a little outside your comfort zone.

4. **Relevant.** Set goals that are meaningful to you and your purpose. For instance, if you set a goal to obtain a degree in finance when your ultimate plan is to be a nurse, the goal is not relevant. A more relevant goal would obviously be to obtain a nursing certification. This is a simplistic example, but hopefully you get the point.

5. **Time-bound.** There should be a limit to all the things that need to be accomplished. More specifically, you need to set deadlines for your goals. For instance, your goal may be to receive a job offer within ninety days. This will also help you track your entire progress, as some goals may have dependencies on others. There will also be a greater sense of fulfillment if a goal is attained within its established deadline.

Take a look at the first letter of each step of the goal formula:

Specific
Measurable
Attainable
Relevant
Time-bound

You did catch that, right . . . S-M-A-R-T? This is more than just a cute acronym to help you remember the steps (although it certainly is, which in and of itself is important). It is also indicative that goals need to be set and followed in an intelligent manner, not just haphazardly.

There is one more important aspect of goal setting that the SMART formula does not specifically address. Goals should be *written* (handwritten or on a computer; it doesn't matter). This should not be ignored nor taken lightly! I do not know all the scientific or psychological reasons why the act of putting goals in writing is so powerful, but it definitely is.

Several studies of goal setting, including large-scale studies conducted by major universities, have proven that people who have committed their goals in writing are more successful throughout their careers than those who do not. I do this all the time and sometimes even take it one step further: I like to sign and date the bottom of the page where I write my goals. This is subconsciously like committing yourself to a contract. Strangely, it works!

To sum it all up, develop goals that are easily measured and can be attained within a limited time, then put them in writing. This will help in determining if the objective is realistic, meaningful, and proven to be worthwhile. You can keep a chart or journal to track your progress and any opportunities that were met along the way. This will also indicate the time consumed and the length of the objective developed. Successfully accomplishing established goals helps motivate individuals or groups toward greater achievements. For you, this means finding that dream job!

Chapter 5 Exercises

Chapter 5 was all about setting goals. By now, hopefully you understand how critical goals are to your short-term and long-term career success. With that in mind, the exercises presented here are just a jump start to get you on track to setting your own personalized goals. Again, a detailed goal-setting workshop is beyond the scope of this book, and I do recommend that you dive into this topic further. Go to www.mycareerfasttrack.com to find a list of recommended resources on this topic.

That being said, do not proceed further in this book until you have at least set some basic goals for yourself. It is often best to think ahead to a long-term goal and work backward, as the end goal dictates the interim steps required to get you there. Remember, when setting goals, make sure each goal follows the SMART formula covered in this chapter; otherwise, your goals have much less chance of being achieved.

1. Where do you want to be in twenty years? This is a long-term goal. What kind of work do you see yourself doing? Do you want to be the CEO of a Fortune 500 technology company? President of the United States? Maybe you want to be retired by then. If you are not sure, think about what is important to you. What do you value in life? What do you enjoy? What are you good at, or what would you like to become good at? Don't be afraid to dream big. You can, and will, make adjustments throughout your career.

2. Where do you want to be in ten years? This is a medium-long-term goal. What kind of work do you see yourself doing? This is an intermediate step in your career and should put you on the path to your twenty-year goal(s) from Exercise 1. For instance, if your twenty-year goal is to be the CEO of a major corporation, perhaps a

good ten-year goal would be to achieve a vice president (VP) role.

3. Where do you want to be in five years? This is a medium-term goal. What kind of work do you see yourself doing? Again, working backward from our example, if you want to be VP in ten years, perhaps a role as senior manager or director is realistic for five years out.

4. Where do you want to be in one year? This is a short-medium-term goal. Your goal may be as simple as settling into a new job and working your way toward a supervisory role.

5. Where do you want to be ninety days from now? This is a short-term goal. Perhaps your goal is to find a new job by then, or at least have chosen your career field with a defined plan in place to get you there. The next chapter will cover this topic in more detail.

6 CHOOSING A CAREER PATH

What I really wanted to call this chapter is, "What do you want to be when you grow up?" That is the ultimate question you should be asking yourself. If you have decided to tackle the process of looking for a new job anyway, you might as well put some extra thought into deciding if your current career field is where you want to be. Perhaps an entirely new career field would better suit your personality, natural skills, and goals. There are several factors to take into account, and I have identified them in this chapter.

Considerations Before Changing Career Fields

Are you unsatisfied with the direction of your current career path (or lack thereof)? If this is the case, perhaps changing career fields altogether would be up your alley. While this is more than possible to do, it is important to first conduct research and carefully consider which career (or careers) may be right for you. Be honest in your assessment. For example, just because you may make a great legal assistant does not necessarily mean that you are qualified to work as a nurse or database administrator.

It goes without saying that not all jobs and career fields are the same. That is why it is important not to make any assumptions. Thinking they know what they are getting into without doing the appropriate research is one of the biggest mistakes career changers make. This is why, before officially deciding to change careers, you must thoroughly investigate each career field that may be of interest to you. This research can easily be done online or at your local library.

Important points that you will want to examine during your research include current and forecasted job outlook, whether the industry is on the increase or in decline, required skill sets, and of course, income potential. I would also recommend speaking to other professionals who currently work in this field. They can tell you what to expect, as well as specific aspects they like or dislike about their work.

Once you have identified one or two career fields that you would be interested in pursuing, you should start searching for open job positions in these fields (We will cover this in detail later in the book.). Do not apply for any of those jobs just yet; this is for research purposes only at this point. Instead, you will want to examine a number of different factors. One of those factors is compensation. For the positions that you would be interested in applying for, is the salary enough to cover your financial obligations and support your family? While some circumstances may allow you to take a pay cut, it is obviously ideal if you do not have to.

In addition to pay, take a look at what the common job requirements are. These job requirements may include education, training, or previous work experience. What is nice about this information is that it is easy to come across. You will find that most job listings will outline all of the requirements needed for the job. This will give you a good idea whether or not you are qualified for the "job of your dreams."

With that in mind, you may want to invest the time to take a few training courses to help improve your training and experience. If you are currently working at another job, that's okay. Many colleges and vocational training institutions offer courses during evenings and weekends, just for working adults like you. Also, the choices in career programs are seemingly endless: information technology, health care, criminal justice, and many more.

If you would like to increase your chances of landing a good job, consider taking a few of these training courses or classes right away. They come in a number of different formats, but they are all designed to help you prepare for a career change. For example, hopeful accountants may learn how to prepare taxes, keep accurate business records, and other practical skills for the job. The length of training needed or required will depend on the career field that you are interested in entering.

If you are interested in using training courses to improve your chances of making a successful career change, you have several options for finding this information, including your local newspaper or the Internet. Many career skills courses are advertised in both locations. You can also simply turn on the television or radio for any length of time. I often see and hear commercials for just such programs.

In addition, you may want to reach out to your local community colleges or vocational centers directly to see what they have available. Yes, you will have to pay to attend most of these classes, but it will almost always be worth it in the end. You may also qualify for certain grants, scholarships, or other financial aid. Either way, hopefully the end result will be a successful entrance into a new career field, namely the career field of your dreams.

Do you want to know a little secret that can launch your career into the stratosphere? Then check out this statement from success guru Brian Tracy, quoted from his blog at www.briantracy.com:

If you read only one book per month [in your chosen field], that will put you into the top 1% of income earners in our society. But if you read one book per week, 50 books per year, that will make you one of the best educated, smartest, most capable and highest paid people in your field. Regular reading will transform your life completely.

I may not have quite read fifty books per year, but when I decided to make a career transition, I definitely followed the spirit of Mr. Tracy's advice. I read roughly ten to twelve books per year in my chosen industry for a couple years straight. As a result, I was able to triple my income in just a few short years. This stuff works; try it!

The bottom line is this: when deciding to change the direction of your career, you must consider (1) what you think you would most enjoy, (2) what your existing skills are, and (3) what skills you think you can obtain in a reasonable time frame. This is a balancing act and worth the time investment in the long run to get it right now.

Matching Your Skills to Appropriate Jobs

Skills refer to the things you do well. The key to finding the best jobs for you is recognizing your own skills and being able to communicate their significance, both in writing and verbally, to potential employers. A majority of the most viable skills are those used in a variety of work settings. These are known as transferable skills.

What are your strengths? What can you do as good as or better than your current or past coworkers? What tasks did you feel most confident performing?

Have you ever earned recognition or rewards for a work-related task? The answers to these questions are indications of your skills.

Determining your skills early, particularly those that are somewhat unique to you, will often help position you as a leading candidate for landing a job. A skill does not necessarily mean it was adapted in a work environment. If this is your first job hunt, and you have no job experience to date, you may still have a chance in the industry.

Many skills, including knowledge-based and transferable skills, can be absorbed and developed as a volunteer, a student, a homemaker, or in your other personal activities. The skills you have used for these activities can be applied to your desired jobs.

Listing and organizing your personal skills could help you more easily fill out job applications, provide useful information for job interviews, and prepare quality resumes. First, you should categorize the skills by separating your interests and aptitudes from your work experience.

1. Aptitudes and interests. These include all of your hobbies, activities in which you have been

involved in the past, and all the things that interest you. By listing all of these, you could examine the skills it takes to achieve each item.

Specific aptitudes and interests may include homemaking, playing basketball, fixing cars, and many other activities. These extracurricular experiences could determine if you are capable of working with a team, able to handle multiple tasks, have viable knowledge of human development, or have knowledge of electronics and the ability to diagnose mechanical and numerical problems. The list goes on, but be sure to consider the skills that would be beneficial for a working environment.

2. Work history. This includes volunteer, part-time, freelance, summer, and full-time jobs. Once you have listed all your past positions, examine the skills you learned in your daily work duties. What did you do well, particularly those things that you may have become known for?

In many cases, job seekers are threatened by job titles and are therefore afraid to apply for fear of having to live up to that title. This should not be the case. As long as your current skills and capacity to learn meet the requirements of the position, your chances of acquiring your desired job increases.

Most Wanted Job Skills

Once you have considered what interests you and where your strengths lie, it is important to understand what potential employers are looking for in job candidates. In today's competitive market, employers are most interested in employees who can contribute to the growth of the company and not just boost its productivity. Hence, most employers tend to look for people who are endowed with the most desirable job skills to match the expectations and necessities of the company.

Here is a list of some important job skills that any job seeker should possess in order to land a good job . . . and keep it! These are in no particular order.

- **The ability to research.** Job seekers should possess the ability to do basic research, not necessarily because they want to land a job in a research company, but to do simple searches on the data needed for a particular activity.

- **Logical thinking.** Most employers need people who are able to produce effective solutions and make sensible decisions regarding a proposal or a probable activity. They also want people who can think on their feet for quick results.

- **Technological literacy.** With the advent of information technology (IT), most job openings require people who are computer literate, or at least know how to operate different machines and office equipment. Most employers do not necessarily require people who are IT graduates. The simple fact that job seekers know the basic principles of technology is often enough. Computer applications such as Microsoft Office (i.e., Word, Excel, PowerPoint, Outlook) are used in most organizations, so this is a good transferable skill to have.

- **Communication skills.** People who are able to land a good job are generally those who are adept in speaking and writing. Employers hire people who are able to articulate their thoughts effectively and efficiently through verbal and written communications. Be concise, delivering all the relevant information as succinctly as possible. Busy professionals, particularly executives and others in senior management, have neither the time nor the inclination to hear you babble or to make sense of your spelling and grammatical error–laden writings.

- **Organizational skills.** No employer wants to hire someone who is disorganized. Organization is extremely important to maintain a harmonious working environment within the company. Hence, most employers find people who know how to arrange schemes and methods that would maintain orderliness in their department and throughout the company. Quite simply, staying organized will allow you to be more productive and will help prevent you from missing work deadlines, which can be the proverbial kiss of death in many organizations.

- **Interpersonal skills.** Because the working environment consists of various kinds of personalities, it is necessary to acquire the ability to communicate with people from different walks of life. This is an important skill, as you will almost certainly have to interact with others in a team environment. This can be difficult at times, because sometimes personalities clash. Learning to look at situations from other people's perspectives can help enhance your own.

- **Professional growth.** Employers hire people who are able to create a plan that will generate personal career growth. This means that the person is willing to improve himself or herself professionally by continually learning new skills. It helps to have clearly defined goals, as discussed previously. If you skipped that chapter, stop right here! Go back and read it now. No joking. Do it!

These are just some of the most desirable assets employers look for in their employees. Hence, it is important for job seekers to take note of these skills to be successful in every endeavor they make. If you find yourself to be weak in any of these areas, move them to the top of your *things to learn* list.

Again, many colleges and vocational schools offer courses in these areas. Some employers even offer them as a benefit to their employees. If this is the case in your situation, take advantage of it. You will get an infinite return on your investment with free training!

In closing this chapter, let's review: You have decided to pursue a whole new career. Perhaps it's because you find yourself in a dead-end career or one you feel no longer suits you; or maybe this is your first *real* career search. Regardless of your motivation, you need to do some research to determine your interests and skills, identify what employers are looking for, and possibly engage in some kind of learning program to enhance your skills in your chosen field.

This is an important, though often tedious, undertaking, but you owe it to yourself to get it right!

Once you have this level of clarity, you will find it much easier and less stressful during the other phases of your job search, including putting together the right "tools." We will cover this in the next section of this book.

Chapter 6 Exercises

In Chapter 6, we discussed several things you should consider when contemplating a new career. Income potential, skill requirements, interests, and experience should all play into decisions you make about the direction of your career. In that vein, the exercises in this section will help you think about some of these items and start journaling the answers.

Documenting your thoughts will help clarify your thinking and will also give you some solid information to reference. This is not a quick process. We are talking about life-altering career decisions that you will have to live with for years to come, potentially. Invest the time to do it right, now, and it will pay dividends later.

1. What kind of career fields are you interested in? At this point, do not think about the income potential. We will get to that, but it is important to think first about what you would enjoy. What fascinates you? It can be anything. It is best to think big and then scale back if you have to. Jot as many ideas down as you want, and remember, only write those things you think you would really enjoy.

2. Once you have made a list of interesting career prospects, narrow the list down to the two that you are most excited about. Now that you have two, think about why you chose those particular career fields. Write down the emotions you experience when you think about them. Also, list the attributes of these careers that cause you to think so highly of them. This could be the travel involved, helping others, the ability to work from home, or a flexible schedule. Why are these careers so appealing to you?

3. Now it is time to take some action, researching your two chosen career fields. Again, stick with

only the top two for now. If, after your research, you find that the chosen careers are not for you, you can go back to Exercise 1 and start the process over. There are many sources for this info. Start with your favorite search engine, and also leverage some of the job search sites such as Monster.com or HotJobs.com. Looking at job postings may be the most revealing. Here is what you want to look for:

- Specific positions or job titles within each field
- Salary ranges for each position of interest
- Daily job duties and responsibilities
- Skill and experience requirements
- Educational requirements (e.g., degree)

4. Based on the information you dug up, start mapping your experience, interests, skills, and salary requirements to the specific jobs available within your chosen career fields. Remember, many skills you may already have are transferable to a variety of jobs. Computer,

writing, speaking, and organizational skills are just a few examples. Did you identify any positions that you feel are a good match for your background and personality? Is the income potential there? If so, proceed to Exercise 5; if not, go back and repeat Exercises 1–4.

5. Once you have identified a few specific positions that are a good fit for you, talk to others who already work in those jobs. If possible, find some individuals new to the industry and some who have been in the industry for quite some time. Also, you want to talk to people who are *successful* in their field—people who themselves are struggling will be of no help to you. Ask if you can have a few minutes of their time to ask them some questions. Most people are happy to help. Find out if the information they provide matches what you found in your research.

6. If you have proceeded through Exercises 1–5 and have some positions you want to go after, now the learning begins. Are you going to need

a specific degree, certification, or license? If so, start researching how and where you can obtain those things and enroll in classes, if necessary.

Look for all the materials you can get your hands on and start learning everything you can about the industry and jobs you are interested in. Learn the lingo. Learn what makes the successful companies and individuals within the industry successful. Learn about the skills you will need to be successful and start developing those skills. If you read just one book related to your field per month, within a year you could be more knowledgeable than many people in the industry. Read one book per week, and you could be one of the top experts in the world in that field.

Step 2
Preparation

Developing Effective Tools

7 THE ART AND SCIENCE OF THE RESUME

A resume is a document that summarizes your career objectives, professional experiences, achievements, and educational background. Your resume represents you to potential employers and serves as your tool to attract attention, get the interview, and ultimately land the job. A great resume will make you stand out from other candidates by showcasing your aptitudes. Think of your resume as your sales pitch; you need to sell yourself in the best possible way.

Review the title of this chapter: "The Art and Science of the Resume." It is so named because writing a resume involves using both tried-and-true elements (science) as well as creativity (art) to uniquely represent you. Since your resume is often the first impression potential employers will have of you, it is worth investing some time and research into the development of your resume. In this chapter, we will discuss some of the juicy details involved in developing what is arguably your most important job search tool, the resume.

Resume Writing from Scratch

Facing a blank page when you are trying to write a resume can be scary and is, at the very least, daunting. You may think that you do not have enough to say about yourself to fill a page. Conversely, you may be wondering just how to list all of your skills and experience within a single sheet of paper. To get started, ask yourself some questions about your past jobs and your career goals.

Before you even begin writing a resume, consider the exact reasons why you need one. While this may sound simple, it takes more than saying, "I want to get a new job." Define your career objective first. Make sure that your goals are specific in terms of industry, position or title, and future professional achievements. Once you are clear on the type of job you are seeking, it will be much easier to compose a resume that highlights your expertise in the area of your interest. If all this seems foreign to you, refer to Part I, "Planning" (Chapters 4–6), of this book, which covers setting goals and identifying your skills.

Once you have your career objectives defined, you need to decide on a resume format. You can create your own, or you can do some research on effective resume formats that may be most appropriate for your industry. Search the Internet or review the resume-writing books in your local library to get a better idea of what well-written professional resumes look like. I am personally not in favor of reinventing the wheel; instead, I find that taking an existing format and putting my unique twist on it works well for me. You can find several good samples at http://career-advice.monster.com/resumes-cover-letters/resume-samples/jobs.aspx.

Chronological vs. Functional Resumes

While there are numerous ways to format your resume, there are two main resume styles, chronological and functional. As its name implies, a chronological resume is one that lists your experience and education in order, starting with the most recent jobs or achievements and ending with the oldest. This type of resume is sometimes also referred to as a reverse chronological resume, because the order of the listing starts with your current employment. This type of resume is generally preferred, as employers want to know what job you currently hold so that they can better assess your qualifications for the job of your interest.

The same is true for your education; your potential employer would rather know your most recent scholastic achievement. Listing your experience and education in reverse chronological order also shows your potential employer your overall career progress. In addition, it helps employers determine the length of employment at each organization and indicates any gaps in your career (we'll talk more about "gaps" later in this chapter).

The chronological resume should list your current job as well as two to four previously held positions. Depending on the industry and relevancy of your previous work experience, most employers want to see at least a five- to ten-year history. Do not skip any employment information on purpose. If your employment history is long, or if you have held jobs further in the past that align well with your current career objective, you can address these qualifications in your professional profile or in your cover letter. Chronological resumes are the most commonly used style, and they work best for anyone who has had some professional experience.

A chronological resume should have the following sections or titles:

- Career Objective
- Professional Summary
- Professional/Work Experience
- Education
- Publications/Special Achievements (if applicable)
- Qualifications/Skills
- References (optional)

Functional resumes focus on your qualifications, not your career timeline. This style of resume highlights what skills you have, rather than where and when you acquired or utilized them. In other words, instead of listing your experiences by your job titles, your resume will contain sections titled by your skills, such as verbal and written communication, customer satisfaction, project management, and so on.

Functional resumes are recommended for college students seeking internships or their first jobs out of college, for those with little or no professional experience, those who have not worked for some time, or for career changers. While potential employers will appreciate the overview of your skills, if you hold any professional experience, consider using the chronological resume, or a combination resume, over the functional format.

A functional resume should have the following sections or titles:

- Career Objective
- Education
- Professional Skills/Qualifications
  (This section should include subheadings as they relate to specific qualifications you want to promote, such as communications, customer relations, or management.)
- Work Experience/History (if applicable)
  (This should include dates, titles, companies, and locations, without listing responsibilities)

- Volunteer Work/Activities (if applicable)
- References (optional)

A combination resume, although not often discussed, has become a popular format in recent years. As its name implies, it is a combination of the chronological resume and the functional resume styles. This hybrid style allows professionals to highlight the qualifications they have that are critical for the job of their interest, while at the same time listing employment and educational history in reverse chronological order.

In my experience, the combination resume style is especially popular in technical fields, such as IT, where many employers like to quickly glance at a list of technical skills, such as a list of specific computer software applications. I, myself, have done this several times. A word of caution: Do not try to do too much when using a combination resume by going overboard with the type and number of sections you include in your resume. It is best to keep the information listed, even in the combination format, to what is relevant for the job.

The previous few paragraphs cover the typical

sections of chronological and functional resumes. Conduct some research on resume styles and find sample resumes from other professionals in your industry. You may need to adjust these headings based on your field, although the content should be consistent across industries. Stick to the basics; do not try to be overly creative merely for the sake of trying to stand out. A professional and polished resume will get you noticed, so do your best to create a resume that is error-free and best supports your career objective.

Now let's touch on some important, yet often overlooked aspects of the resume.

Writing an Effective Career Objective

In general, you should start your resume with a career objective. Often listed as simply "Objective" on your resume, a career objective is a statement of your career goals. It sounds simple; you want to get a good job, utilize your experience and education, and get paid well. However, this is the most difficult part of the resume to compose, as you are limited to one to two sentences in which you are expected to convey your professional expertise, expectations from a job and an organization, as well as goals for your professional growth. Doesn't sound so easy now, does it?

The most common mistake people make is not listing an objective. Most people operate under the assumption that the objective is not necessary to include in a resume because it states the obvious; your objective is to get the job you are applying for. However, this is a big misconception. Employers are looking for an objective; they want to know what it is that you are looking for to determine whether or not you are a good match for their company.

The second most common mistake is including a career objective that does not actually express your goals and your qualifications. For example, a statement like the one below is commonly used in resumes:

> *To obtain a position where my experience and education can be utilized and expanded.*

If you examine this statement, you will find that it does not say anything specific about what the person is looking for in terms of professional growth. Avoid using generic statements like this. They will hurt you more than help you in your job search, because your employer will be left with the impression that you do not have a set goal in mind.

Now that you know what not to do, here are some helpful tips on creating a winning career objective that will get your resume noticed and get your foot in the door. Think of your whole resume as a sales tool; your career objective is your opening statement. First, make your career objective personal. You want potential employers to know what *you* want, not just restate what other people want.

Second, you want to state your commitment to your career goal. If you are unsure of what you want, how are employers to believe that you really want the job at their organization and you are not just applying because you want to get out of your current work environment? Do not be afraid to state what you want from a job and from an organization.

Third, while you want to state your commitment, you also want to show that you are willing to take action to achieve your goal. Indicate what direction or action you are willing to take to accomplish your career objective.

The fourth, and most important, factor in a successful career objective is being specific about what you are looking for in a work situation. While you can say that you are looking for a "challenging" environment, this does not mean anything to employers, as people define challenges in various ways. Avoid using generic and broad terms. Simply state what you want and what you are willing to do to get it.

Keeping in mind these criteria, let's revise the above career objective statement so that it effectively states what you want.

To obtain a position of a sales representative in the health insurance industry, where I can utilize my management and customer relations skills, with the opportunity for performance-based advancement.

This statement tells a potential employer that you know what kind of job you want, what experience you have to help you get the position, and what you are willing to do to become a successful professional within the company. Thus, you have just created a winning career objective for your resume.

Writing a Professional Summary

As we have discussed, in today's competitive job market, employers rely on well-written resumes to screen potential candidates. In many instances, employers look through job search websites, such as CareerBuilder.com or Monster.com, to find professionals with the skills, education, and experience that fit their needs. These employment search websites, along with many companies' own online applications, require candidates to upload their resumes to express interest in a specific opportunity.

Without an opportunity to send a personal e-mail or cover letter, you have to make sure that your resume expresses your personality, in addition to listing your professional and educational experiences and achievements. To do so, you can include a professional profile or summary at the beginning of your resume that allows you to market yourself through a narrative. This section allows your potential employers to learn something unique about you and your career, as well as get a good feel for your communication skills.

To write an effective summary, you should first understand what information should not be communicated in your resume. While a summary provides an insight into what is unique and competitive about you, it is not a place for you to indicate any personal information that does not relate to your career. Information such as ethnicity, marital status, sexual orientation, religious beliefs and affiliations, and so on, should be left out of your resume. While this information certainly is descriptive of who you are, it is not relevant to potential employers to prescreen your qualifications for their opportunity.

Additionally, the summary should not contain your previous professional experience unless you can clearly demonstrate how such background can be of value in your future career development. Beware of generic statements such as “I am well organized and detail oriented.” Employers want to hear your unique voice and get a sense of your communication skills while reading the summary portion of your resume. Using generalizations about your abilities will make employers believe that you are either a poor communicator or are using such statements to fill up space on your resume.

Your summary should be in the form of a short paragraph or bulleted statements, containing only a handful of sentences. I prefer using a short paragraph, but other options are valid. There isn't a sentence limit, per se, but as a general rule, do not take up more than one quarter of the page. Your summary should begin with a headline that summarizes your professional title or your professional statement. Emphasize your title by featuring the headline in bold and larger font, as it allows your potential employer to grasp who you are quickly. Here are a few examples:

Financial Planning Professional
Technical Support Specialist
Advertising Account Manager

It is important that this title is well crafted, as it is the first impression your potential employer will have of you.

There are three areas a well-written summary should address:

1. Your experiences and skills as they relate to your ideal job
2. What you can bring to the organization and the open position that no other candidate can
3. Your professional goals

There is much disagreement about the narrative style that should be used when drafting your summary. Some suggest the use of third-person narrative to avoid "I" and "me" statements, which can make you seem self-absorbed or braggadocious. Others argue that the use of third-person narration in describing one's own experience and accolades gives your document a distant tone. One resume expert once told me, "This isn't a secondhand account of your experience, like a biography; therefore, a removed narrator should not be looking in and profiling your career from the outside. This rhetoric raises questions about accuracy and needs to be cleaned up to boost and solidify your professional image."

A third option is to use neither a first-person nor a third-person narrative, as you will see in the example that follows. My personal opinion is that if you are submitting your resume to an employer directly, it is probably best to either use a first-person narrative or no narrative point of view at all. If a third party, such as a placement firm, is submitting your resume to an employer on your behalf, as is common in the information technology field, they may restructure your summary in the third person. This is fine. At the end of the day, it is the content that really matters, and I have used all three styles with equally successful results.

Regardless of the style you choose, be sure to reinforce your title, and sell only the experiences and skills that meet your career objective. If you have multiple career objectives, such as you wish to get a position in either marketing or public relations, develop separate resume summaries for each of the objectives. Again, this is about maintaining focus and clarity.

The professional summary should also include a "Core Competencies" section. This section can be presented in various ways, but it is generally best when presented as a bulleted list. Core competencies are more than just technical skills; they are your strong points, your foundation, your *core*! To be effective, they should be industry-specific and operations-oriented. Among several important uses, this section acts as a keyword-rich area that enables your resume to be quickly found by HR technology. An example of an effective summary would be as follows:

Successful financial planning professional with over fifteen years of personal and retirement planning experience. Managed a small financial planning firm, achieving double-digit financial returns for all clients by developing personalized investment portfolios. Leader in the development and professional growth of other financial planners through effective and motivating mentoring strategies. Motivated by the opportunity to leverage this background to help grow a budding financial services firm and provide leadership and strategic market direction.

Key competencies include:

- *Personalized portfolio development*
- *Financial forecasting*

- *Retirement portfolio management*
- *Development of ongoing professional growth strategies*

Much like your overall resume, your summary should be well written and error-free. Make sure to review your summary and customize as necessary for the various opportunities of interest. An effective summary will help you *hook* your employer. It should sell you as a primary candidate for the job, leaving your employer with a great first impression of you.

Effectively Stating Your Work Experience

While you may be able to easily describe your job responsibilities to your friends, listing them in a resume and showcasing how your experience meets your career objectives can be difficult. To get started, you must first consider what type of job you are seeking. Just as your career objective and summary should reflect your professional goals, your current and past experiences must showcase that you are the best candidate for the job you are applying for.

To accomplish this, it is imperative that you successfully highlight your achievements. Remember that a resume is intended not only to provide the reader with a comprehensive presentation of your background but also to be an easy-to-read navigational tool that allows the reader to never lose sight of your major accomplishments.

In listing your professional experience, try to focus on those responsibilities that indicate that you are qualified to take the next step in your career. Due to the fact that more and more companies, as well as job search sites, use scanning software to pick out candidates, it is important that you use keywords, including active verbs, to describe your skills. Instead of beginning your job descriptions with "Responsible for," try to use active verbs such as:

- Managed
- Developed
- Created
- Communicated
- Interfaced
- Achieved

These keywords get straight to the point of describing your responsibilities, which is exactly what the employers are looking for. Choose these words carefully. Do not say that you "managed a project," implying you were responsible for the whole task from start to finish, if you were only responsible for communicating the project to other associates. Instead, state that you "Developed and executed the communication strategy for associates," describing your role more accurately and emphasizing your strengths.

Typically, the first job listed on your resume is the one you currently hold. In this case, make sure that your responsibilities are stated in present tense, as you are still responsible for them. For example, say "*Manage* accounting activities" instead of "*Managed* accounting activities." This will indicate to your potential employer what your day-to-day activities are like and how they complement the responsibilities of the position for which you are applying. All previous jobs should be listed using past tense and should start with active verbs such as *managed*, *developed*, *accomplished*, and so forth.

Additionally, make sure the responsibilities you are listing are relevant to your career objective. List only those responsibilities that help you put your best foot forward. For example, if you are looking for a job that requires managing a team of people, focus on your development and participation in group projects instead of focusing on solitary activities such as filing paperwork.

Now that you know what elements should be included in the work experience section of your resume, let's discuss how this section should be formatted. It is best practice to separate each position with a blank space or two to clearly delineate jobs. Each job listing should include the company name with city and state, as well as dates of employment. These are typically displayed on a single line. You should also include your title, followed by a brief summary (single paragraph) of your job duties. Finally, for maximum impact, add a section that includes a bulleted list of key accomplishments.

It is important to ensure that each job you list contains all these elements as described. If you mix your duties with your accomplishments into one text-filled blob, the impact of each is watered down. Employers read the summary, then check bullets for outcomes and results that may relate to similar circumstances they are currently facing. If they skim bullets and see task-based material, rarely do they keep reading.

Finally on this point, if the resume looks overwhelming, with a lot of words and poor formatting, they will likely discard it; thus, it is important that your resume is formatted with enough white space and does not contain any errors. Here is an example of a well-formatted job description:

***ABC Company**, St. Louis, MO, 5/2006 to Present*
Help Desk Technician
Assist customers in resolving diverse hardware and software issues. Ensure quick resolution of customer concerns and escalate more complex support issues to senior technicians and engineers.
Key Accomplishments

- Reduced customer callback rate by 25% through accurate identification of root causes of technical issues and consistent implementation of appropriate solutions.
- Earned “Help Desk Technician of the Year” award for comprehensive technical knowledge and outstanding customer service in 2009.

Listing Certifications and Licenses

Your resume is a compilation of your professional life, from your education to summer internships, from publications to technical skills. It is critical that your resume include anything that will help you get the job that you are interested in. Most professionals make the mistake of focusing on experience and education only. As a result, they disregard any additional information, such as certifications they have in their field, that would enhance their qualifications and ensure that they stand out from the competition.

Any professional certifications and licenses that impact your career and your ability to do your job should be listed on your resume. This concept is straightforward for those professionals who cannot actually perform their jobs without having a license to do so, such as teachers, real estate agents, and medical professionals. If you are in a profession that requires specific certifications or licenses, your resume should contain a section specific to this information. The heading should state “Professional Certifications” or “Professional Licenses.” List here any certifications and licenses that you have acquired in your professional experience.

Additional consideration is necessary if your professional field does not require certifications or licenses. How and where this type of information is listed, if at all, is important to think about. For example, having a certificate from a seminar on project management may not be required for you to do your job effectively. However, such a certificate can be helpful in virtually any field, and if included on your resume, it can help you catch an employer's attention. This is particularly true in high-tech fields.

In fact, in the highly competitive field of IT, some certifications are almost expected for certain positions. If listing a certification or license can help your chances, include it. If it is completely irrelevant and cannot help you, it is just noise and should be left out.

Consider any courses or training seminars you attended in your professional career. Do not forget to include any courses you may have taken as part of the training at a current or previous job. For example, if you have completed a course on using Microsoft Excel spreadsheets as part of the training on your current job, and you know that you will be required to work with this program in a new position that you are seeking, make a note of this on your resume.

Treat the list of licenses and certifications as you do your professional experience; make a list, in reverse chronological order, and consider which of the items you listed are relevant to your professional goals. Give the date when the certificate or license was obtained. For example, if you took a course over time, indicate the completion date in form of month and year only. The exact name of the certificate or the license should be listed, along with the issuing organization. No additional information is necessary for this area of your resume. Further, make sure to highlight any certification and licenses in your cover letter if they promote your qualifications for the job you are seeking.

If the list of licenses or certifications is lengthy, you can include this information on a separate sheet of paper. Your resume should list a few of the most recent items; however, if the listing exceeds five items or so, indicate on the resume that a complete list is available on a separately-attached page. Your resume or your cover letter can point out this information, as well as highlight those elements that promote you as the best candidate for the job.

Okay, okay, so this chapter is a little longer than the rest. I get that, but as I said, your resume is the most crucial tool in your arsenal. You have one chance to make a first impression, and it deserves the investment of time. Hopefully, I've presented some helpful tips to get you started.

Remember, if you get stuck, be sure to review some of the samples provided on professional job websites. If you do not want to take any chances, hire a professional who has experience writing high-impact resumes. Not all resume writers are created equal, so before you hand over your hard-earned cash to one of these folks, be sure to review some of their previous work. Pore over each section of their sample resumes and filter it through the best practices listed in this chapter. This is too important to take a gamble on!

Chapter 7 Exercises

Before you jump into the job search, you need to be prepared and have the right tools, particularly a resume. A well-written resume can go a long way in helping you land a great job, and that is what the exercises in this section focus on. Take the time to go through each of the exercises and complete them one at a time. Use the chapter as a reference while going through the exercises to help keep you on track. If you get stuck, don't be afraid to reach out to capable professionals or online resources for help.

1. Do you have a resume that you have used in the past? It doesn't matter if it is old and outdated at this point. If you have one, locate it,

regardless of whether it is a paper copy or digital. If you don't have a resume, proceed to Exercise 3.

2. Once you have found your old resume, read through it in detail. Compare it to other well-written sample resumes, and also measure it against the suggestions we discussed in Chapter 7. How does it stack up? Identify things you like and dislike about it, and highlight areas you would change.

3. After you have finished poring over your old resume, start creating a new one. You can use Microsoft Word or any other capable word-processing software. Format it according to the suggestions made in Chapter 7, and use other sample resumes as a guide. For the content, simply copy the "good" stuff from the old resume so you don't have to re-create the wheel. Where applicable, you may have to make some changes or write new verbiage to make the resume as high-impact as possible.

4. If you do not have a resume or want to create a brand-new one, find some well-written samples online or obtain them from other people you know. Just make sure they follow the format and best practices provided in Chapter 7. If it is an electronic copy, even better. You can simply copy and paste this into a new document and use it as your outline. Obviously, you will want to replace the content of the sample resume with your own so that it is personalized.

5. Once you have completed your new resume, review it and review it again. You may want to step away from it for a while, maybe even overnight. When you come back to it, you may have a new perspective. Make sure your resume follows the suggestions provided in Chapter 7. Have others you trust take a look and provide feedback. If you really want to do it right, have a professional resume writer review it and make some changes to give it extra polish.

8 COVERING THE COVER LETTER

So, you have finished your resume and you feel like you are ready to start pounding the pavement (or keyboard, if you are searching online). Not so fast! Before you send out your resume or resumes, you will want to take a close look at your cover letter. For starters, are you even using a cover letter? If not, you will need one, and we will discuss what this entails in this chapter. If you have one, keep reading anyway to ensure your cover letter contains all the necessary elements.

Before we discuss what your cover letter should contain for employers to take notice and review your resume, it is critical to understand the importance of having a cover letter. One of the most common mistakes in job applications is not including a cover letter. If you are e-mailing your resume, the cover letter can be included in the body of the e-mail or attached. If you are faxing or mailing your resume, assure that the cover letter comes before the resume.

Omitting a cover letter from your job application appears unprofessional to your potential employers. Having a well-written, personalized cover letter allows employers to get an insight into who you are, how you communicate, and how you present yourself as a professional. This is a big deal!

When it comes to creating the perfect cover letter, there are a number of important factors to take into consideration. One of those factors is the job that you are applying for and the specific requirements of that company. It is not uncommon for some employers to list exactly what they want cover letters to include. If you are given a sample or directions, follow them. Not following instructions can result in your resume, as well as your cover letter, ending up in the *do not call* pile.

Why would a company have its own instructions as to what to include in a cover letter? Because no two companies are exactly alike. That is why it is advised that you do not use the same cover letter for each resume that you send out. Instead, create and distribute different cover letters for each employer to which you are submitting your resume. You can have a sample cover letter or a template to use as a reference, but you should take the time to personalize each cover letter.

The cover letter should be customized appropriately for the jobs that you are applying for and the companies to which you are sending your resume. For instance, if you are applying for the position of a legal secretary, you will want to plainly state that position. This will automatically set you apart from a good percentage of your competition. Customizing each of your cover letters to the particular jobs that you are applying for is a great way to get yourself noticed, as you took a few steps that many others may not have.

Besides being customized, the perfect cover letter is brief and to the point. At the same time, it should not be so brief as to leave out relevant details. A cover letter should be at least three paragraphs, but keep it under one page long.

As for what to include in your cover letter, you should highlight a few of your skills and qualifications. However, be advised, I am not recommending that you simply cut and paste from your resume verbatim. Be original and find creative ways to restate some of your most important qualifications that you believe uniquely position you as the *perfect* candidate for the job. It is also important to keep this portion of your cover letter short and to the point. Your resume will go into further detail, but it is still best to quickly outline the qualifications and skills that you have.

Be sure to focus on those that relate directly to the job that you are applying for. For example, if you are applying for the position of a legal secretary, summarize your computer software knowledge, typing skills, transcription skills, and so forth. Leave off irrelevant skills. For instance, small engine repair, crane operations, and chemical engineering are not applicable to a legal secretary position.

With today's use of technology, it is advised that you do not use any colored fonts. Black ink is preferred. It is also advised that you do not use colored paper for your cover letter, or resume, for that matter. This is a big paradigm shift from even just a dozen years ago.

Before the Internet and e-mail were commonly used for resume transmission, we used fax, snail mail (traditional post office mail, complete with envelopes and stamps), and even sneaker-net (delivering it in person). With this manual way of delivering and reviewing resumes, I would often use special resume paper with fancy borders as a way of enhancing the professional look and to catch people's attention. I found this to be highly effective.

Today, most resumes are captured electronically into databases automatically over the Internet or even scanned in manually. Either way, these systems often have difficulty with extracurricular *features* such as borders and colors, and they may reject your resume. What used to help you can now often hurt you!

Cover Letter Must-Haves

Here are some great tips on composing a winning cover letter to accompany your resume:

- Address the letter to the appropriate person. A mistake that many job seekers make is not taking the time to address their cover letter to the appropriate person, such as the recruiter or the hiring manager. Take the time to address your cover letter to the appropriate person. If the job description does not include a person as a contact, take a cue from the text and address the letter to the team listed as the contact. Using generic lines, such as "To whom it may concern," is not recommended on a cover letter. It is too impersonal.

- Know the goal of your cover letter and express it clearly and concisely. Sell yourself in the best possible light, making sure that you sound confident and professional in your cover letter. Concentrate on the positives, and highlight those qualifications that make you a perfect candidate for the job. Even if you are insecure about some of your qualifications or feel that you may be slightly underqualified for the job, put your best foot forward.

- Customize your cover letter to the position you are applying for. As we have already covered in detail, it is important that your cover letter address why you are the best person for the particular job you are seeking. This includes indicating the job title in the cover letter. Generic statements, or statements indicating that you are interested in any open position within the company, make you appear not only unprofessional and unprepared, but also desperate or as if you do not really know what you want.

- Answer these two questions: why do you want this particular job, and what can you do for the company? These two questions must be addressed in the cover letter to let your employer know that you are serious about your interest, you have considered the opportunity and how it fits with your professional goals, and you are willing to bring your skills and experience to the table to benefit the organization you want to work for.

- Proof your cover letter. Errors and misspellings leave a poor impression on the employer. Almost all word processors and e-mail programs have spell-checking capabilities—use them! Enough said.

- Close the cover letter by indicating to your potential employer when you intend to follow up on your application. Do not end the letter with a statement that leaves it up to the employer to call you at their convenience. Let the employer know that you want to follow up, along with when and how you will do so. This confirms your interest in the position and your professional etiquette. Note, you must follow up when and how you indicated on the cover letter or you will lose credibility, and maybe the job.

Common Cover Letter Mistakes

Just as there are elements your cover letter should have, there are several items that you must avoid to get through the first round of resume review and move one step closer to getting the job that you want. Some of this is simply counterpoints from the previous section, but is important enough to restate so there is no misunderstanding. These are common mistakes you don't want to make:

- Addressing the cover letter using a generic greeting or misspelling the name of the personal contact or the company. The address line is the most prominent part of the cover letter. It should be included even if the cover letter is sent via e-mail. Generic greetings are not recommended, as they make it seem like you have a template for your cover letter and you simply send it to all employers you are interested in working for. Do the research and find out who the appropriate contact is for the cover letter. Then make sure that the person's name and the company name are spelled correctly. If your address line contains errors, your cover letter may never make it to the hiring manager.

- Telling the company what they can do for your career. Simply stated, employers care about your qualifications and what you can do for the company. Do not spend your time merely focusing on how working for them would be great for your career. While that may be true, it certainly is not what the employers want to hear . . . to a point.

It is acceptable to state that you are looking for a position that provides mutual benefits for you and the company. But by and large, potential employers want to hear how you can benefit their team. They want to know what you can bring to the table that is innovative and focused on results. Make sure that your resume lets your employer know just why you are the best candidate for the job.

- Repeating your resume. Do not go over the information that is in your resume in your cover letter verbatim. Your cover letter is meant to entice and provoke the employer to review your resume in great detail. Restating the information in your resume does not address what the employers want to know, which includes why you are the best candidate for the job. Highlight certain areas of your resume, but do so in the context of your career goals and how such qualifications benefit the company.

- Starting every sentence with "I." While your cover letter is about you, starting each sentence this way will make your employer believe that your communication skills are not up to the level of your professional background. Discuss your qualifications, your goals, and your professional attributes—what you have to offer the company.

- Asking employers to call you at their convenience. The most generic closing statements in cover letters ask the employers to contact you at their convenience. If you are truly excited about the opportunity, you do not want to wait for them to call you back whenever they feel like it. Instead, close your letter by letting the potential employer know that you will contact them, as well as the manner in which you will do so—and then *do* follow up. This shows your interest and your take-charge attitude. This is not an invitation to bug them daily. Use discretion with regard to how you will follow up and how much. No more than weekly, and preferably biweekly, is recommended.

I hope that this section has enlightened you to the importance of including a cover letter when submitting your resume. More specifically, I hope you have grasped the suggestions provided here so that your cover letter will be well written, thus increasing your chances of landing the job of your dreams. Of course, I would be remiss if I did not provide you with a resource that provides sample cover letters. With that, you can find several samples at http://career-advice.monster.com/resumes-cover-letters/cover-letter-samples/jobs.aspx.

Admittedly, not all of these samples follow perfect form, as we have discussed in this chapter. Most are fairly well written; however, I would challenge you to read through several of the samples and see if you can point out the strengths and flaws of each. Use them and customize them for your needs.

This will save time from completely starting from scratch. Combining this cover letter with your resume will create a powerful impact on potential employers and put you ahead of much of the competition.

Chapter 8 Exercises

Every resume you send to a potential employer should be accompanied by a cover letter. A well-written cover letter will have hiring managers salivating at the opportunity to not only read your resume but, more important, meet you in person. While the core of your cover letter will likely remain consistent, it should be customized, where applicable, to each position you are applying for. The idea here is to make each employer feel like you put your best foot forward, that you really want the position, and that you are uniquely qualified for it. The exercises presented here are similar to those you used for your resume (Chapter 7).

1. Do you have a cover letter that you have used in the past? If so, find it now. If not, proceed to Exercise 3.

2. Once you have found your old cover letter, read through it in detail. Compare it to other well-written sample cover letters, and also measure it against the suggestions we discussed in Chapter 8. What's good and what needs improvement? Identify these areas, and highlight what you would change.

3. After reviewing your old cover letter, start creating a new one. Format it according to the suggestions in Chapter 8 and use other sample cover letters as a guide. For the content, copy the good stuff and ditch the not so good. Where applicable, you may have to make some changes or write new verbiage to make the cover letter as high-impact as possible.

4. If you do not have a cover letter or would like to create one from scratch, find some well-written samples online or obtain them from

other people you know. Just make sure they follow the format and best practices provided in Chapter 8. Copy and paste this into a new document and use it as a template. Again, replace the content of the sample cover letter with your own so that it is personalized.

5. Once you have completed your new cover letter, review it a few times, stepping away from it for a while, if possible, and approaching it from a fresh perspective. Make sure your cover letter follows the suggestions provided in Chapter 8. Have others you trust take a look and provide feedback.

Step 3
Searching

Hitting The Streets

9 IT'S WHO YOU KNOW

If you find yourself in a position where you absolutely must find a new job, particularly if you are under a time crunch, you should try to identify resources to help you reach your goal as fast as possible. Aside from the usual suspects, such as job search sites, it is also helpful to ask for information from the people on your warm contact list. These are people you already know and are some of the best resources you can leverage.

Warm contacts can provide you with up-to-date information on the company and position vacancies that are not posted on job ads. If they cannot provide you information about the specific job that you are looking for, they may be able to refer you to a person they know who might be able to tell you something about the job.

This is called networking. Networking is when you start using your warm list to get information or referrals to their other contacts. Many people are repelled by the thought of networking. Some believe that it is not a reliable source of information about the job. Others say networking is more difficult than following the leads on the ads that are posted in the newspaper or on the Internet. I say that networking is the single most effective way of finding quality career opportunities. There is often less competition, and you have a greater chance of landing a job when you were directly referred to someone at the employer.

One of the biggest mistakes job seekers make is not leveraging their contacts to assist in their job search. Don't be afraid to ask for help. It is not uncommon for job seekers to conceal the fact that they are unemployed out of embarrassment. This is a critical mistake that costs them valuable job opportunities.

Contrary to popular belief, networking is not that difficult to do. It is often as simple as calling or meeting with someone you know and obtaining valuable information that can help in your career search. Also, since the people you meet may belong to the same industry, they can provide you information about positions that are not advertised and firsthand facts about the company.

You may be networking already and you just do not know it. When you have seen a job posting by a company you know little about, you ask your friends if they know somebody who works for the company. That's networking! Even if you are not thrilled by the idea of networking, it is still essential when seeking a job. To make networking easier and more productive, this chapter offers a few tips.

Prepare Your Warm Contact List

When you have prepared your warm contact list, it will be easier to select the people whom you prefer to call first. These are the people you think have some information about the job. They usually have firsthand, up-to-date, and reliable information. Who may be included in your warm contact list? Here are a number of selections.

- **Relatives and friends.** These people are always willing to help you in your job search or business venture. They will be able to provide you information if they have it or refer you to trustworthy people who will be able to help you. If they will introduce you to some of their contacts, they can surely provide honest information to you regarding the person you are going to associate with.

- **Members of your church, political party, social club, or fraternity or sorority.** You probably did not expect it, but people who share the same faith, beliefs, or hobbies may also help assist you with your job search. You may have a different career from theirs, but they might know someone who is in the same field or will be able to help you in your career. Their opinion can sometimes help you in making a strategy on how to approach and ask for help from their contacts. However, depending on your level of association with them, they may think twice about giving their opinion or thoughts about their contacts. Don't be offended if they opt not to help you; this happens sometimes.

- **People who sell you things.** You may think that your relationship with these people is purely based on exchanging money for goods and services. However, people who sell you things are also sources of information when networking. Since these vendors sell their goods to a variety of people, they may be associated with someone who belongs to the same field as you do or may have heard information about your target job from their other clients.

  These people will also be happy to help you, since they know that maintaining a pleasant relationship with you means a stable business for them. In addition, your having a good job means increased purchasing power for you, thereby increasing the chances that you will purchase more from them.

- **Former employers, colleagues, or coworkers.** Maintaining a good relationship with previous employers and colleagues has more benefits than you can imagine. This is the reason smart employees try their best to iron out any difficulties with their previous employers even if they are no longer associated with the company. Aside from the possibility that potential employers will call your previous employers when they review your job history, former employers and colleagues are also a good source of information related to that field.

When you ask for help from family and friends, there is the possibility that the information they give you is secondhand, from another source. They may not be able to give you firsthand information or detailed accounts unless they work in the same field that you came from or would like to go into. This is different when you consult former employers and colleagues from the same sector. They will be able to provide you with valuable information and may be able to clarify such information and answer your questions.

- **Members of your professional organization.** If you belong to a professional organization related to the field in which you are looking for a job, you can consult the organization for current postings made available by its members. If you do not belong to any, consider joining one since this will be beneficial to your career growth. A professional organization can provide you unbiased information on current job openings from its members. The organization can also give you details on the company profile and even on current market and career trends.

The types of contacts represented in this section are the most important people you should include when creating a list of targeted warm contacts. It is better if you contact them all so you can have as many options in your job search as possible.

Calling a Warm Contact

When you call warm contacts, inform them that you are actively seeking a job. Ask them to let you know if they hear of job openings you might be interested in. It is better to inform them of what type of job you are looking for. Also, do not forget to leave your contact number with them so that they can get in touch with you if they hear of anything. Better yet, leave a copy of your resume with them so they can show or submit it to someone who will be able to help you in your job search.

Assess Yourself Before Calling

Your warm contact may ask about your skills, experiences, abilities, interests, expectations, and career goals. You should be able to talk about these sincerely, and you should be able to describe what information you would like to have from your contact. To help you prepare, you can practice by drafting a script of what to say. That way, you can clearly articulate what you would like to communicate to your warm contact. This is often referred to as an "elevator pitch," and sales and marketing professionals commonly use this technique to tell people about their products and services.

Your elevator pitch should be brief, to the point, and compelling. Practice your elevator pitch so it naturally rolls off the tongue. Also, anticipate questions about yourself. Practice answering questions about your previous job and what you can contribute to the company. This is like preparing for an interview "lite."

Ask for Referrals

If your warm contact is not able to provide you information that will be helpful to your job search, ask for the names of at least two people who may be able to help you. Ask for their contact number and, if possible, the time they will be free to talk over the phone.

Contact Referrals Immediately

When warm contacts give you referrals, they may even call the referrals to inform them that you will be asking for more information. Sometimes, the person you were referred to will call your warm contact to follow up. Therefore, it is best to call your referrals within a few days after you have spoken with your contact.

When you make a call, introduce yourself and inform your contact of the person who referred you and how you are related to that person. Be polite, but straightforward, in informing the person what information you are seeking.

Networking is not difficult. With enough practice

and experience, you can maximize the benefits that you can get from networking. This should be a key component of your job search and one of the first things you do. Many job openings are never advertised and are filled through word-of-mouth referrals. Tapping into this will provide more opportunities and can kick your search into high gear!

Chapter 9 Exercises

Starting in Chapter 9, we began discussing tactics for finding job leads, specifically creating a personal network. Simply put, you need to start working your contacts. Analogous to fishing, the more lines you have in the water, the better your chances are of catching a fish. By leveraging the eyes and ears of as many people as possible, this extends your reach and increases the number of job leads you have. The exercises in this section will help you identify your contacts and build a network to help you find a job.

1. Pull out a pen and paper, or open a new document on your computer. Make a list of all the people you know: relatives, friends,

colleagues, acquaintances, fellow members of your church or other civic organizations, and so forth. This is a lofty exercise and may take some time, but the idea here is to identify as many people as possible whom you can start speaking with about job leads.

2. If you have spent some time on Exercise 1, you should have quite a list going. Now, we want to create a "circle of influence." Use a pencil and paper to draw a target (bull's-eye) shaped figure. The innermost circle is the core. Inside the core, write the names of the people on your list to whom you are the closest. This will likely be your family members and maybe close friends. After all your closest contacts are listed in the core, move to the next circle out and write the names of other friends and colleagues you know relatively well but who may not be "core worthy."

   Continue this pattern, moving outward and listing those with whom you are less familiar as you go along. Get the idea? Close people in the center, acquaintances toward the outer edge.

3. Develop an elevator pitch about yourself. This should be a thirty-second blurb that provides a high-level idea of your skills, experiences, abilities, interests, expectations, and career goals. An example would be something like this:

   I am looking for a job where I can use my twenty years' experience and industry certifications in computer network administration to help support a growing organization in the health care industry. I consider myself a people person, so I am especially interested in a position where I can work in a team environment. My initial goal is to start as an individual contributor, but my long-term plan is to move into a management role. Teaching and mentoring others is something I enjoy and is important to me.

4. Once you have identified your list of contacts and have developed your elevator pitch, it is time to start smilin' and dialin'. Reach out to as many people as you can, starting with the core

and working your way out in the circle of influence. Sending an e-mail, or perhaps a Facebook message, is okay, but this often takes away from the human element.

Make it a goal to reach as many people by phone or in person as possible. Tell them exactly what you are looking for and why you feel you are qualified for such a position. No one can sell *you* like you, so be passionate.

Don't forget: Be courteous and gracious. Thank each person for his or her time, then follow up with a letter, e-mail, or other message. In your follow-up, thank the person again and reiterate your elevator pitch.

5. Ask each person you speak with for referrals. There are many types of referrals. It could be a hot lead directly to a hiring manager for a specific job opportunity, or it could simply be the name of a person who knows someone in the industry you are interested in. Either way, follow up with these referrals right away.

   Where possible, ask the person who gave you the referral to make a warm introduction, even if it is just an e-mail to the referral in which they drop your name and suggest that you will be reaching out to them. Definitely do not let these leads go cold. At best, you may miss good opportunities; at worst, you may burn a bridge with the referral or the person who referred you. You can't afford this!

10 THE POWER OF THE INTERNET

In the past, applying for a job meant looking through the classified ads in the local paper. The advent of the Internet has allowed for a number of different options, making it easier for someone to find a job, even in another state or country. It has made the world a smaller place, with everything at one's fingertips and just a click away.

If properly leveraged, this technology can make your job search much more efficient and stress-free. If this is the first time you are turning to the Internet to help you find a job, you will definitely want to continue reading, as this information is likely to be quite an eye-opener for you. If you have used the Internet in your past or current job search, there may be some new tips, tricks, and techniques to help take your search to the next level.

Career Search Websites

As previously mentioned, when it comes to using the Internet to help you find a job, you will discover that you have a number of different options. These options include websites that are commonly referred to as job posting or career search websites, company websites, as well as the online editions of your local newspapers. Examples of popular job search sites include Monster.com, CareerBuilder.com, and TheLadders.com, but there are many, many more. It is advised that you use career search websites or job posting websites to your advantage. In fact, these days it is important that you do so.

Most job sites will require a person to create an account, fill in certain information, and upload a resume. Most of the popular sites are free for their basic services (i.e., posting resumes and job searching), but some do charge a fee. As with other, more traditional methods of job hunting, many of the same rules apply with regard to the information required for submission—contact information, education, background, references, and so on.

One of the key reasons career websites are so highly recommended is that they are easy. For starters, you can find a number of career search or job posting websites by performing a standard Internet search. Try it: just open the search engine of your choice (I like Google, but that's just a personal preference), and in the search field, type "job search websites." Then hit the enter key on your keyboard or click the search button on the site. Thousands of results will come up.

Aside from being easy to find, you will also notice that most job search websites are pretty easy to use. Sites like Monster.com have been around for several years and continually make improvements to enhance the end-user experience. In fact, many career sites provide step-by-step "wizards" to guide you through the process of establishing an account, entering your personal information (only that which is relevant), uploading or creating a cover letter and resume, and searching and applying for jobs. If you miss something important, you are often alerted to this fact. Online help is also generally available to answer common questions.

Equally important, you will find that most job

search websites (at least the good ones) are customizable. What does this mean for you? It means that you can tailor your searches to the criteria that are most relevant to you. For instance, you can search for all available job listings within a certain distance from your home. You also often have the option of further filtering your search by industry or specific job titles. As an example, you could do a search for all cashier jobs in the retail apparel (clothing) industry that are within ten miles of your zip code. This ability to customize your search allows you to be much more productive, as you do not have to sift through job postings that are not relevant to what you are looking for.

One of the most powerful aspects of many career search websites is their automation capabilities. This takes *customizable* one step further. Once you have entered your search criteria, you often have the ability to save these searches so that you can do the same search as often as you would like without having to reenter the search criteria over and over. This is a big time saver! Even better, though, you can elect to have the system automatically run the search for you each day and e-mail you the resulting job postings. While I do not recommend relying 100 percent on this technology, it does allow you to be a little less *hands-on* so that you can spend more time on other important job search activities, like networking and interviewing.

In addition to allowing you to actively search and apply for jobs, many job search websites allow you to post your resume online for free. This feature is nice, as it also enables some level of automation. Allow me to explain.

Just as you can search for and apply for job postings, employers can conduct searches for resumes that contain keywords that match the skills they are looking for. For instance, an IT company may want to find a local application developer with experience in Microsoft Visual Studio. By searching for keywords such as "Visual Studio," they will be presented with a list of potential candidates that have "Visual Studio" listed on their resume. Should hiring companies like what they see, they have the ability to contact these candidates to request further information or to set up a phone screening or face-to-face interview.

There is one caveat to keep in mind: if you are not careful, you open yourself up to the possibility of your current employer finding your resume online. This probably isn't a good thing. To avoid this, some job posting websites provide a privacy feature that hides your name and your current employer's name. This allows you to screen potential employers before revealing your identity.

That being said, I have been contacted about several job opportunities this way, some of which I accepted, so it definitely works. Personally, I keep my resume up-to-date and searchable on my favorite sites at all times. I recommend doing this for a few reasons.

First, you never know what kind of curveballs life will throw at you and when you may need to find a new job, especially these days. Maintaining a pipeline of potential job leads is good career insurance, so to speak. Second, sometimes the best job offers come when you are not expecting them. In fact, a couple of my jobs came about in this manner. I was not actively looking and was contacted out of the blue because my resume was current and available online.

As a sidebar, let me also mention that when you are not *desperate* to find a job and are in a position where you could take it or leave it, you have the most leverage to negotiate your compensation package. If for no other reason, it is good to keep your resume online and *fresh* at all times because it allows you to see trends in the industry. You will gain an understanding about things like, who is hiring, what skills are in demand, and what the going pay rates and benefits are. This is like doing preemptive, automated research. Use it to your advantage.

It may go without saying, but when posting your resume or submitting it to a specific job listing online, proceed with caution. As soon as you click “send,” you may find that you are unable to make modifications later. This is typically not the case for resumes saved on sites like Monster.com or CareerBuilder.com, but some sites are not as sophisticated, so you have to be careful.

In keeping with the “cautious” theme, you generally cannot recall an e-mail that has your resume attached to it. For that reason, make sure that all of your information is accurate before you submit your resume or application. The first impression employers or recruiters often have of you is your resume.

Submitting a resume that has grammatical and spelling errors says, “I am sloppy and unprofessional, and I don’t care enough about my career, let alone this job, to put my best foot forward." That may seem like hyperbole, but many hiring managers and HR professionals look at it this way. If hiring managers have two potential candidates, and all else is equal, they will pick the one they believe is more conscientious and detail-oriented. With all the competition for jobs these days, it is worth the extra time to do it right the first time.

Furthermore, if you are e-mailing your resume, you should examine each company's policy first. Some companies request that you do not submit your resume as an attachment, in fear of viruses. This may require you to copy and paste your resume into the body of an e-mail message. If you must do so, review your resume to ensure that the original formatting integrity is maintained. Conversely, some may require that you submit your resume as an attachment so they can easily print or upload the file into their own systems. You just never know, so pay attention and do it their way.

Company Websites

As mentioned previously, you can use companies' websites to examine job openings. You can usually find a company's website by performing a standard Internet search for that company. Many companies have the jobs for which they are hiring, as well as information on those jobs, listed on their websites.

Even if you are unable to find any companies that are hiring this way, you may be able to sign up for free job alert e-mails. These e-mails will notify you when a new position comes available. While this may not happen for a few weeks, months, or years, you have nothing to lose by doing so.

Social Networking

Do not forget the power of social networking when looking for new career opportunities. Websites like Twitter (www.twitter.com), Facebook (www.facebook.com), and LinkedIn (www.linkedin.com) can give you instant access to a huge network of folks who may be able to help in your search. While many dismiss such sites as childish or a waste of time, you should not underestimate their potential. Not only can you quickly get the word out to others who can refer you to specific job opportunities, but there are also topic-specific groups that may be able to offer creative ideas and suggestions that you had not previously thought of.

If you are going to leverage the power of social networking tools for your job search, and I suggest that you do, make sure your profiles are appropriate for this task. Inappropriate pictures, off-color jokes, and any other content that could potentially be construed as offensive will generally kill any chance you may otherwise have had. I also recommend that you use a clear, professional-looking photo of yourself as your profile picture.

Try to complete your profile with as much info about yourself as possible that may help your cause. This is especially important for LinkedIn, which is designed to be a professional networking tool. On this site, you can essentially build an online version of your resume, which becomes part of your profile. All this content is searchable by search engines, such as Google or Yahoo!, and can help you get discovered more easily.

Finally, be proactive in your use of social networking tools. While companies can, and sometimes will, find you, do not sit around waiting for this to happen. Take the initiative to search for peer groups and industry-specific groups on these sites that you can be a part of. Get involved; get to know other individuals and actively participate in online discussions. Not only will this increase your chances of others finding you, but also it may provide you with some warm contacts you can leverage in your job search.

While the information provided in this chapter is not an exhaustive accounting of all the details of online job hunting, the intent is to provide a few points you should remember when using the Internet to help you find a job. Just use your best judgment. The same rules that apply for traditional job searching methods generally apply online as well. If a career opportunity that you find online looks too good to be true, it just may be. Do your research and be vigilant.

Chapter 10 Exercises

Leveraging the power of the Internet was the focus of Chapter 10. As you have hopefully seen, there are many ways you can utilize the Internet to your advantage. If you use an "all of the above" approach, this will increase your chances of finding good job leads. Therefore, the exercises in this section will get you on the right path with regard to using the Internet in your job search.

1. If you haven't already done so, start reviewing some of the popular job search websites that are available. There are many, with Monster, CareerBuilder, and TheLadders being among the more popular. Once you are familiar with at

least a couple of these sites, create a profile on the sites where you can upload your resume or build one online. Don't forget to use the search tools to look for specific opportunities that may be of interest to you. You are generally able to apply for these jobs directly, but at the very least, you should be able to obtain the contact information to which you can apply. Again, this will take some time, but it is worth it for the amount of exposure you can get.

2. Do you know of some specific companies that tend to hire individuals for the position you are seeking? If so, visit their websites. If you don't know their web address, a simple Internet search should turn it up for you. Many company websites have a "careers" or "jobs" page on their website. Some are as sophisticated as allowing you to search and apply for positions right on the site. Other sites may just give you the contact information to whom you may submit your cover letter and resume. Either way, give it a shot. Just make sure you are submitting your resume only to

jobs for which you are genuinely interested. It's impolite to waste other people's time, and you shouldn't want to waste your own either.

3. If you have a Facebook, Twitter, LinkedIn, or other social networking account, don't be afraid to reach out to these online communities to help get the word out. Update your status message and, where appropriate, send messages directly to specific individuals in your online network, explaining exactly what you are looking for. Just be careful: if you have "friends" or "connections" whom you may not want to know of your job search, you will have to be more discreet about how you send your messages.

4. If you haven't already done so, be sure to sign up for a LinkedIn account. While it can be classified as a social networking site, it is specifically designed as a professional online network. The goal isn't to tell the world every personal detail about your life; it is used to connect and keep up with professional business

contacts. LinkedIn has things called "groups," which are smaller subcommunities that focus on a specific topic. Search for some groups that are applicable to the industry, or even the job, you are looking for. Become a member of these groups and get involved. These more intimate communities can be a great source of job leads . . . but don't forget to reciprocate!

5. Once again, follow-up is key. Keep track of all the positions to which you have applied. If you have not received a reply regarding a job application, reach out to the appropriate people after a week or so. It may be too soon for them to have made any decisions, but at least you are showing your interest and may earn yourself a closer look. If they say that they are still looking through applications and haven't come to any conclusions yet, ask if it would be okay if you followed up with them again in a week or two. As always, be polite and thank them for their time and consideration.

11 TRADITIONAL SOURCES

In a society where we have become dependent on the Internet, many job seekers automatically turn to career search websites or job posting websites. While these online resources are a great way to find job openings in your area, they are not your only option. It's hard to imagine that less than two decades have passed since Internet access was the exception and not the norm. Job seekers had to rely on traditional resources and processes to search for jobs. We will explore some of these resources in this chapter. You may find them to be valuable in your job search.

Newspapers

At the risk of sounding contradictory with some of my earlier comments, the employment section of your local newspaper may still be a feasible resource for some. It depends on where you are in your career and what type of job you are looking for. With all that technology flying around out there, why is the newspaper still a valid job search tool?

Although many businesses have started using the Internet to their advantage, believe it or not, not all have. This means that there may be a great employment opportunity in your area, but the company behind that opportunity may choose not to use the Internet or may not even know how to use the Internet to list that job online. You do not want to take the chance of missing out on any high-paying jobs, do you? Since your answer is likely "no," you will want to examine your local newspaper and its employment section.

Another reason you may want to use your local newspaper to search for a job is that the job openings, and often the companies looking to fill them, are local! If you live in a large city or near one, you may have multiple newspapers to choose from, each of which likely focuses on a particular area. If you have your hometown newspaper, you may be able to tell what businesses are the ones with listed jobs. This can sometimes be difficult to do online, yet it can be a big help, as it can prevent you from applying to companies known to have a bad track record with paying or treating their employees poorly.

Ease of obtaining the local newspaper (or newspapers) is just another of the many reasons to consider using the employment sections to help you examine all open jobs. There are multiple locations, possibly even thousands, that likely sell your local newspaper. In fact, you may even get home delivery. This means that you may already have a newspaper in your possession or one will soon be delivered. If this is the case, you will want to open it and start examining all job listings right away. Since newspapers are so easy to obtain, you do not have to go out of your way to examine the job listings inside.

Should you decide to use the Internet in conjunction with your local newspapers, you will want to examine any online editions of your newspapers as well. While not always, many newspapers have separate classified advertisements, including employment listings, for their online editions and their print editions. This means that you may be able to find additional local job listings by using the

Internet in conjunction with your local newspaper.

No matter how you locate a job lead, you may find that competition is plentiful, as hundreds or thousands of job seekers may be applying for the same position; so it is that much more important that you do what you can to stand out in the crowd. Make sure you have a well-designed cover letter and resume and that you follow all the submission instructions to a T.

Unless the ad explicitly instructs you otherwise, follow up on your application after a few days. Be courteous, professional, and persistent, but do not be a pest. Chances are the company literally has a huge stack of resumes to sift through. If you follow this advice, the newspaper may be a decent source of a job lead or two.

Job Fairs

An often overlooked method of job searching is job fairs. This may be because many job seekers get annoyed with the jam-packed, full-of-activity, and baffling series of events that go along with job fairs. Others may feel that their chances of success in this type of venue are limited due to the large amount of competition. Nevertheless, job fairs can be an effective way to find a job, because many companies participate in these events. From my experience, many job fairs are geared toward individuals who are early in their careers or are looking for entry-level positions; however, some are industry-specific and may provide opportunities for more experienced professionals.

Job fairs are not as daunting as they may seem. The important thing is to be properly prepared and maintain a high level of organization. Here are some of the things that a job seeker must have by the time he or she is at the job fair to make the most out of it:

1. Do your homework. Your goal as a job seeker is to find the best employment possible; hence, it is important to do some advance research before going to a job fair. Usually, the organizers of this event will post the companies that will participate in the job fair. Obtaining some information about the companies and the positions they are hiring for gives you an edge over your competition.

2. Take resumes-o-plenty. It is important for job seekers to have a large supply of resumes before going to the job fair. In this way, the applicant

will be able to provide resumes to all of the potential employers in the job fair. The more applications you deliver, the better your chances of landing a job. Not to mention, you do not want to have to tell one or more potential employers that you are "fresh out" of resumes. This will make you seem unprepared–bad juju!

3. Dress for success. As they say, first impressions last; hence, to be a cut above the other job seekers, you should learn how to impress employers by dressing your best. Clothing should project a professional outlook, enthusiasm, and the determination to get the job you really want. Dress for the job you want, not the job you have.

4. Be ready to deliver. Many companies have hiring managers or human resources personnel onsite at job fairs. Just as job seekers are competing for jobs, employers are competing for qualified talent. By doing their initial screening onsite, they can shorten the hiring cycle. Be ready for this; look your best and be

sharp, just as you would if you were attending any other job interview.

5. Maintain a list of companies you apply to. Many employers want to know about other positions for which you have applied. They do this for a couple of reasons. One, they are nosey and curious about who their competition is. Two, they want to see how consistent you are. If you are applying for similar positions other places, this shows that you have a solid goal for the type of position you are seeking and likely the required skill set. If you are applying for several unrelated positions, this indicates that you do not know what you really want and may be desperate to take anything. This may, in fact, be the case, but you do not want them to know that.

Knowing these best practices can be helpful, especially for those who have never attended a job fair before. If this is you, it is definitely worth your while to attend one, particularly if you are new to the workforce. Even if you do not walk away with a job offer on the spot, you will likely walk away with knowledge about the industry and job market, a list of names of potential employers, and perhaps even some contacts. Job fairs can also be a good practice ground for some of the skills you are learning in this book and hopefully other sources.

Department of Labor

Although it may be more than possible for you to find and apply for jobs on your own, consider seeking assistance wherever and however possible. For many individuals, that assistance means leveraging the services of a recruiter, but did you know that you might be able to get assistance through your state's Department of Labor?

In the United States, all states have a Department of Labor, or some variation of this name. This labor department is able to assist individuals like you with a number of work-related issues, including finding employment. Although this may not be the first resource many individuals think of, if you are struggling to find work and want another angle, consider contacting your state's labor department.

One of the many benefits of seeking assistance from the labor department is the options available.

These options will depend on the state you reside in. For instance, in New York, you can visit your local labor offices or you can use their job-searching website. The ability to use a website is ideal, especially if you are currently employed, as you may be unable to visit your state's labor offices during the daytime. The Internet gives you twenty-four-hour access!

Another advantage of using your state's labor department is the job bank they have. "Job bank" is a term regularly used to describe the list of job openings that the state has access to. You may be surprised with what you find. Many employers, especially those that are locally owned and operated, choose to advertise their openings only through a state labor department. What does this mean for you? It means that you may search high and low and still be unable to come across the same job openings that your state's Department of Labor can help you find.

Further, using the assistance of your state's labor department increases your chance of being awarded a job. Once again, you will find that it all depends on the state in which you reside; however, if you apply for jobs through your state's labor department, you are not able to apply for just any job. One of the many reasons employers trust the judgment of state labor departments is that they aim to send prescreened, qualified applicants for interviews. This increases your chances of getting a job, as you are less likely to spend your time applying for positions that you may not be the perfect candidate for. This is similar to the benefits of working with a private recruiting firm.

If you are interested in seeing what your state's labor department can do for you, do it—you have nothing to lose. Most states offer free assistance to those seeking employment within their state or county lines. You can easily find the contact information for your local Department of Labor offices by doing an Internet search or by using the telephone book.

Chapter 11 Exercises

With modern technologies such as the Internet being so prevalent, it's easy to forget that there are other ways to look for a job. Not that many years ago, local newspapers and job fairs were the main job-hunting tools available. This was the topic of Chapter 11, reintroducing you to some of the traditional resources that can still be used in your job search. This is also the objective of the following exercises.

1. When was the last time you opened an actual paper newspaper? With the constant stream of news available online, for some it has been years. Strive to change this today. Buy the major newspapers available in your area. Turn

to the "Employment" or "Help Wanted" section. You should find an exhaustive list of job openings there. You may have to go through dozens or hundreds of jobs that aren't applicable to you, but when you come across an ad that interests you, circle it. After you've found one or more ads, follow the instructions provided to submit your resume or application. You may find that the ad ultimately directs you to a website to complete your application.

2. Look for upcoming job fairs in your area. You can find these advertised in the newspaper, online, or on the radio or television. Regardless of how you find it, plan on attending. As suggested in Chapter 11, make sure you are adequately prepared. Try to get an idea of which employers will be present and research those you are interested in. Print several copies of your resume. Get a haircut. Have your best business attire pressed (and altered if it doesn't fit quite right). When you are there, take advantage of every opportunity to meet and

speak with individuals who can help you find good job leads.

3. Research your state's labor department. There should be a website available with helpful resources and information about how your state can assist you in finding work. You may experience varying degrees of success, depending on your state, but it's another *line in the water*. If your state's labor department has offices in your area, they may be able to help you write a resume, obtain job training, and use job placement services. Most states' websites even allow you to search for jobs online. Do a search now, and identify potential jobs to which you can apply.

4. As always, follow up on those jobs to which you have applied to show continued interest and to keep your name at the top of the list. Of course, be courteous and thankful for the company's time.

12 NONADVERTISED JOBS

To this point, we have covered several commonly used sources for identifying job opportunities, such as the Internet (e.g., job posting websites) or the employment section of your local newspaper. While these are important and productive ways of finding available jobs, many successful job seekers choose to submit resumes to companies who are not currently advertising available jobs. This may come as a surprise, but many job openings are not publicly posted. In fact, I would submit that *most* of the highest-paying jobs across virtually all industries are never advertised at all.

In many cases, hiring executives, particularly those who are well connected, prefer to hire individuals who have been referred to them by a trusted source. This reduces some of the risk of hiring someone off the street whom they have never met or know nothing about. Still others simply let the *go-getters* come to them on their own initiative.

There are definite benefits to submitting your resume for nonadvertised positions, but there are also some caveats to doing so. Before examining the pros and cons of submitting your resume to a company that is "not hiring," however, you may be curious as to how you can go about doing so. When taking this approach, many job seekers use two different tacks.

In today's society, many businesses have websites. These websites may give the mailing address to the company in question. There are many job seekers who will submit their resumes to that address in hope of seeing success. Others will simply mail or drop off their resumes or job applications to companies in their area using an address they know.

There are a number of pros, or positives, of applying for nonadvertised jobs. One such positive is the jump start you can give yourself. Many companies will choose to take out job advertisements when they have open positions, but others will just go through their current pile of resumes and job applications. If you play your cards right, one of those resumes or job applications may be yours.

Another pro is the impression that you may create of yourself. Many employers view the proactive submission of your resume as a show of initiative. This is the type of impression that you want to create for yourself. You want a prospective employer to be pleased with your desire and need to have a job, namely with their company.

While there are a number of positives to applying to nonadvertised jobs, there are some caveats to doing so as well. As previously stated, most employers view the submitting of a resume or a job application as showing initiative, but you may be surprised how others feel about the same action. It is possible that some companies would view your submission of an unsolicited resume or job application as spam if you do not approach it right.

To reduce the risk of leaving this type of impression, you need to be focused on what you are looking for and to whom you submit your resume. Never simply submit a generic application to the employment (human resources, HR) department, saying you are willing to take whatever they have to offer. At best, this makes you seem desperate and unfocused. At worst, they will view this as *spam* and immediately dismiss your application.

As we have discussed in previous chapters, know what you want, what your strengths are, and the areas in which you can add value. Once you know this, submit your resume directly to the department manager who has hiring authority. If you do not know this person, do some research: call the company and ask, use the Internet (including the company's website), or if available, ask one of your contacts who may know.

Another of the downsides to applying for nonadvertised jobs is the response time. As previously stated, many companies choose to go through their pile of job applications and resumes. One of these job applications and resumes can be yours, but you never know when you may end up getting a call for a job interview. You could receive a phone call in a few weeks, a few months, or even a year later. This may not help if you are looking to find a new job now. With that in mind, you have nothing to lose by submitting your resume or job application anyway. You may be surprised with a quick response time.

As outlined above, there are a number of benefits and caveats to submitting your job application or resume for a nonadvertised position. Since the decision is yours to make, you will want to proceed with caution, making sure your intentions are clear. That is why you should take the above-mentioned factors into consideration before committing to this approach.

To conclude this chapter, I will present a case study, a little-known secret of sorts, that I have successfully used to land a good job. To start, I had to decide what type of position I was looking for. Once I knew this, I had to figure out what types of organizations might employ for such roles. Specifically, what type of industry was I looking for? When I did this, I was looking for a corporate sales position in the IT industry.

The next challenge was to find a listing of these organizations. At the time, I used my local library, as it provided free access to a database of all organizations in my local metropolitan area. These days, you can easily find this information on the Internet. In any case, this tool organized these companies by what is known as SIC codes. Standard

Industrial Classification (SIC) codes are four-digit numerical codes assigned by the US government to business establishments to identify the primary business of the establishment. For more information about SIC codes, you can refer to http://www.siccode.com/about.php. Once I found the SIC code for my desired industry, I was then able to do a search for all organizations listed under that specific SIC code.

The resulting list was quite fruitful, as it provided the company name, address, phone number, website (if applicable), owner/president/CEO, number of employees, and annual revenue (if available) for each organization. I was able to print this list and take it home with me. From there, I crossed out those on the list that I felt did not meet my criteria (e.g., size, revenue, and location).

After I had my final list, I researched the companies to the extent possible so I could customize my cover letter for each submission. Then I printed my resumes and cover letters. I hand-addressed the business envelope and addressed it to the owner, president, or CEO, whichever name was provided on the list. I printed and neatly trifolded the cover letter and resume together, sealed them within the envelope, and mailed them.

All told, I spent *a lot* of time and made quite an investment in postage, envelopes, and fancy stationery, but it paid off. Within a couple of weeks, I received a call from the vice president of sales at the largest Internet service provider (ISP) in the area at the time. He expressed that he and the CEO of the company were impressed with the professionalism of my resume and cover letter, as well as my initiative. He also said that my timing was perfect, because the company was getting ready to start an aggressive expansion plan and needed solid individuals to fill sales roles. I interviewed with him in person less than a week later and walked out with the job. Because the job had not been advertised, I was even able to negotiate my salary. Score!

Chapter 12 Exercises

Chapter 12 invoked some “outside-the-box” methods of searching for a job. The truth is, many jobs are never advertised; rather, they are filled through word-of-mouth referrals, someone who knew someone. This harkens back to Chapter 8, “Networking for Success.” Still, some people, myself included, have had success finding jobs through unsolicited, direct contact with individuals who have the authority to say yes. This can be a matter of proper timing and a little personal sales and marketing skills. Yet, anyone can make this work with enough effort. The following exercises will put you on the right track.

1. If you haven't done so, go back to Chapter 8 and complete the exercises contained within. If you've already done this, congratulations! You are free to proceed to Exercise 2.

2. Get online and browse http://www.siccode.com. Use this tool to identify the SIC code for your chosen industry or industries. There may be several SIC codes applicable to your industry. Make a list of all these codes and keep them handy.

3. Now, go to http://www.sorkins.com or find other business listings that allow you to search for companies based on SIC code. Many of these websites charge a fee for their service, but you may be able to find some free ones. If nothing else, you may want to check with your local library, as some have a subscription to Sorkins or similar services and may allow you to use it.

   Once you have turned up a list of companies, peruse the list of names to make sure you have the results you are looking for. If so, send a cover letter and resume to the companies you are interested in. Be sure to send this as a hand-addressed, stamped envelope to a specific person. If no other name is provided, send it to the president or CEO. Sound bold? I did this, and it worked—I got the job!

4. It shouldn't come as a surprise at this point, but don't forget to follow up and be polite.

13 THE POWER OF POLITENESS . . . AND FOLLOW-UP

Okay, I'll admit it: although "being nice" is not necessarily a job search tool, it is still a critical element to keep in mind while going through the job-search process. As you conduct your job search, you will come into contact with a number of different individuals, likely from a number of different companies. No matter whom you are dealing with, it is important that you are polite at all times. It sounds so obvious, but you would be amazed how many people take simple acts of chivalry for granted these days. Do not make this mistake!

One of the best ways to understand the importance of politeness is to put yourself in someone else's shoes. For starters, imagine yourself as the hiring manager for the position you are applying for. If you were to come into contact with two job applicants, one of whom responded with "please" and "thank you" and another who acted as if speaking to you was just a waste of his or her time, which individual would you be more likely to hire? Most likely, you would respond to the candidate who was polite. It is no secret that employers do not want to hire those who are impolite or have bad manners.

One of the many reasons it is important for companies to hire polite and compassionate people is that their employees can either make or break their business. This is particularly true when direct customer contact is required. Companies want and need employees who are warm, welcoming, and inviting. An employee with a poor attitude can cause customers to take their business elsewhere.

Be polite at all times and to *whomever* you meet. Unfortunately, many job seekers do not heed this principle. Many mistakenly believe that the only person they need to impress is the individual conducting the job interview.

Yes, your attention and politeness should be focused on your job interview, but courtesy should be part of your everyday character, not an event. For instance, should you drop off a job application or a resume, greet the acceptor in a pleasant and positive manner. It is not a stretch to believe that employees pass word on to their supervisors about poor experiences they had with those dropping off applications or resumes.

Should you receive a call asking to schedule an interview, there is a good chance that the supervisor conducting the interview will not be the one on the telephone with you. Often, assistants or secretaries handle these types of scheduling tasks. This should not impact your behavior or demeanor when making the appointment–whether you are dealing with a secretary or a hiring manager, treat everyone with the same level of respect. Regardless of rank, title, or pay grade, we are all human beings.

If that's not enough reason, consider that secretaries often have the ear of the hiring manager." Answering another telephone call, not saying "thank you," or otherwise acting rudely will likely kill your chances of getting the job. You have too many other obstacles to be creating your own in this way.

Follow-up

As discussed, one of your main goals through the job search process is to make a great first impression. If you've spent hours developing a killer resume and cover letter and weeks finding a hot lead to submit your resume to, the last thing you want to do is let it slip through the cracks. Once you have thrown your hat into the ring for a potential job opportunity, it is important to follow up. A simple follow-up is the professional and polite thing to do and can only increase your likelihood of receiving a callback.

This may sound trivial and obvious to many, but this is a foreign concept to others. Submitting your resume or application should not be the end of your efforts. These days, good jobs are too scarce to leave to chance. After you have applied for a position, you should contact the employer to ensure your application was received and, if possible, find out what the timeline for next steps is (i.e., the interview).

Not only does this help keep you informed of the details, but it also provides a couple of other benefits. First, it shows the employer that you are truly interested and that you take the position seriously. Employers want to know that the candidates they are considering really want the position, as this leads them to assume that you will work hard and do a good job if hired. The other benefit of following up after applying for a job is that it can potentially score you some advance one-on-one time with the hiring manager or HR representative. Often, just a call is enough to get your resume moved to the top of the stack.

So, when and how often should you follow up? There is probably not a single "silver bullet" answer to this question. Common etiquette is to generally wait about a week after submitting your application before following up. This is enough time not to seem desperate, but soon enough to display your interest in the position.

If a job posting has a deadline for resume or application submissions, you should probably wait about a week after this deadline before following up. Of course, if the posting explicitly states "no calls," then you should respect this and be patient for a callback. If you know someone at the organization, this person may be able to do a little reconnaissance and provide you with some insight about the status of your application. This is where those networking skills come into play. Just don't do anything that would get this person in trouble or kill your chances for the position.

In terms of frequency of follow-ups, I would definitely suggest no more than once per week, and possibly ten to fourteen days. Even then, I would ask for permission to follow up again after the initial call. Say something like, "I understand that a decision has not been made yet. Would it be okay to follow up with you again in two weeks if I haven't heard from you by then?" This shows that you are persistent but respect their time by not trying to be a pest.

In this chapter, we discussed a couple of best practices to follow during your job search. We discussed the importance of politeness and professionalism, and took this a step further by creating a simple follow-up strategy. As a reminder, politeness comes in a number of different sizes, shapes, and styles. In most cases, saying "please" and "thank you" should be enough for those of importance to take notice. As basic as this may seem, if you follow these simple practices, this can give you an advantage over other candidates.

Step 4
Interviewing

Selling YOU

14 PREPARING FOR THE BIG MEETING

At this point in the process, you have undoubtedly invested an enormous amount of time, energy, and perhaps even money assessing your goals, conducting research, picking the career that is right for you, creating your resume and cover letter, and sending it to several potential employers. Then it happens. You get a call from a potential employer who wants to set up an interview.

Whether you are a newbie or seasoned job hunter, you may be a bit nervous about upcoming job interviews. If you are, you are definitely not alone. The good news, however, is that there are a number of steps you can take to prepare yourself for success. If you are well prepared, you will be more calm and confident; and confidence (or lack thereof) definitely shows during a job interview.

One of the most important, yet often overlooked, steps you will want to take is to research the company where you will be interviewing. This is a piece of cake if the company has an online presence, and these days most companies do. You can impress your interviewer if you know about the company, even just a little. Researching each company that you have an interview with should not take more than an hour or two. The basic information, such as the goals of the company and where their main headquarters are located, is often enough to grab the attention of your interviewer; however, the more you know, the better.

Another of the many steps that you can take to make a good impression at your next interview involves researching common job interview questions. There are a number of books and online resources available that provide a list of common interview questions. Just do an Internet search for "common interview questions," and you will see what I mean. Familiarizing yourself with questions that you may be asked, such as those regarding your strengths, weaknesses, goals, and so forth, can help improve your response time, as well as ease any nervousness that you may have.

In addition to familiarizing yourself with questions that you may be asked during a job interview, you may want to hold a few practice or mock interviews. These practice sessions can be done in front of a mirror, or they can be done with the assistance of a close friend or family member. Treat all job interview practice sessions as if they were the real thing, answering each question in a professional manner. You will get much more out of the practice if you take it seriously. (See Chapter 15 for more on this topic.)

Another step you can take to prepare for an upcoming interview involves printing a few extra copies of your resume. This makes you look prepared, in more ways than one. Although interviewers should already have a copy of your resume on hand, it wouldn't hurt to ask if they would like to see a new copy. Also, you never know when you may be asked to meet with others in the organization while you are there.

Many times in my career, when I have gone in for an interview, the company has sprung an extra surprise interview or two on me. When this happens, it is a good thing, as it indicates that the employer obviously has interest in you. It can also shorten the life cycle of the hiring process, as you are getting more interviews done at once. Now that you know this is a common practice, do not let it surprise you; be ready for it!

You should also take along a pen (two pens actually, in case one is lost or does not work) and a notebook. Use this to take notes and jot down answers to questions you ask during the interview. Once again, this shows that you are serious about finding a great job and indicates that you will go to great lengths to obtain that job.

If you really want to score some extra brownie points with the interviewer, come prepared with a list of intelligent questions that you can ask during the meeting. I'm not referring to questions like what the company does, where their headquarters are located, or any other information that is easily obtainable by doing basic online research. I mean put the pressure back on them, to a point. Do not go out of your way to make someone feel ignorant or uncomfortable by any means. It is, however, advisable to ask specific questions about the company and position, such as:

- I read the job description posted online, but could you please describe the perfect candidate for this position in your own words?
- I noticed that your product revenue has steadily decreased while your services revenue continues to grow. Is this an indication of a change in the strategic direction of the company?
- If I accept this position, is there an opportunity for career advancement within the company?
- Once you have selected me to join the team, what can I do immediately to help you be successful?

These are killer questions, and believe me, prospective employers eat this stuff up. Specifically, notice the presumptuousness of that last question. This may seem a little "forward" to you, but hiring managers appreciate candidates who know what they want and are not afraid to make it known. Just do not come across desperate or arrogant. Make it clear that this is just as much of an opportunity for you to screen the company as it is for them to screen you.

The above-mentioned steps are just a few of many

that you can take to prepare for an upcoming job interview. Additional preparation includes mapping out the route you will take to the interview site, arriving early for your job interview, and properly thanking people for their time. A high degree of preparation can do you no harm; only good!

Chapter 14 Exercises

In Chapter 14, we discussed several ways you can prepare for a job interview. Preparation is important! Professional interviewers can definitely distinguish well-prepared candidates from those who are "flying by the seat of their pants." With all the hard work you undoubtedly did to get the interview, it is worth it to take a little extra time to sharpen up for it.

It takes a lot of effort to build credibility, but it can be blown in minutes if you try to "wing it" and fumble your way through the interview. You are better than that! Now you have a chance to practice and prove it to yourself. Let's dive right into the exercises for this chapter.

1. If you have an interview already set up, or if you are anticipating getting an interview with one or more specific companies, do some research on them. These companies, almost certainly, have a website. If you know the URL (website address), go there now. If not, do a basic Internet search for the company name. Once you have found the site, go through every page on the site, particularly focusing on the "About" page. Your goal is to learn everything you can about the company: products, services, locations of operation, industry awards, history, and so on.

2. Find some common interview questions. You can use books or the Internet. Most interview questions attempt to key-in on your background, experience, goals, talents, weaknesses, problem-solving ability, character, ability to work well in a team environment, and so forth. Your job is to have prepared answers ready for the actual interview. This will help your confidence and ultimately allow you to provide smooth, well-articulated responses.

3. Come up with your own list of questions that you would like to ask the employer during the interview. I provided some examples in Chapter 14, and again, you should be able to easily find more examples on the Internet. Don't go overboard and ask thirty questions. Pick five to ten that are most relevant and have them pre-typed or written in a notebook so you can write the answers and other notes on the pages during the interview.

4. Print multiple copies of your resume, along with your prepared list of questions that you will ask during the interviews. Place them in a folder so the pages do not get bent, dirty, or lost. Have a couple of pens ready inside or clipped to the folder. You may also want to print a few key pages of information from the company's website and have them available in your folder, too. You can use this for extra, last-minute studying while you are waiting for your interview to begin. It can also be a nice reference during the interview and will make you seem prepared.

5. Going through practice interviews is another great way to prepare. Chapter 15 is dedicated to this topic. You will find corresponding exercises at the end of that chapter.

15 THE BENEFITS OF MOCK INTERVIEWS

While we briefly touched on this topic in the previous chapter, I feel it is worth covering mock interviews in more detail. So, when was the last time that you had an interview? If it has been a while, you may want to consider doing a few practice runs. These practice runs are commonly referred to as mock interviews. Although mock interviews may seem a little silly, there are a number of benefits to doing them.

One good thing about mock interviews is that there are options. Many job seekers try to use their friends and family members for practice. If you decide to take this approach, have your partner ask you common job interview questions. You should have these already prepared if you did the exercises in

Chapter 14.

Questions should focus on topics such as what your strengths and weaknesses are, why you want this job, why you feel you are uniquely qualified for the position, and so forth. Be sure to answer with professional responses, just as you would in a real job interview.

You can also do a mock interview in front of your mirror. While this approach is not as realistic, it can help you practice your intended interview questions. It also helps you adjust your facial expressions and body language.

Reassurance is another benefit of doing mock interviews. It is no secret that job interviews can be nerve-wracking. Even if you have had other job interviews, they can still make you nervous. Many job seekers find that practicing with their friends or family members helps ease this nervousness. In fact, many people feel an increase in confidence, having practiced first.

Yet another benefit of mock interviews is that they force you to prepare for the real thing. This preparation may include answering common interview questions in a timely matter, giving a proper greeting, as well as departing properly from a job interview. If this is your first job interview, or if you have not attended a job interview for quite some time, you may be unsure as to how the interview will proceed. Such guidance will not only calm your nerves but can also help your next job interview go more smoothly.

If you are able to do a mock interview with a close friend or family member, you may get a number of pointers. Using other individuals, especially those known for their unbiased opinions, is the best way to examine your job interview approach.

If your friends or family members have any suggestions, such as tips on how you can improve your answers, try them out during your practice. You may find the suggestions to be just the answer you were looking for. To add an even more realistic feel to the mock interview, you may find it helpful for the practice interviewers to come up with some of their own questions that you haven't practiced. This will help you think on your feet.

These are just some of the benefits of doing mock interviews with a close friend or family member. You can also practice in front of a mirror, but you may have the best luck with someone who can give you feedback or provide you with helpful suggestions. In either case, try to make a video recording of the mock interview so you can review it later. You may be surprised by what you can learn about yourself.

Chapter 15 Exercises

The focus of Chapter 15 was practice interviews. Like anything else in life, the more you practice, the better you'll get. The benefits are enormous, as you will make a better impression, deliver your answers with confidence, and be less nervous. (I say "less" because it's natural to be a little nervous—I still am!)

1. If you haven't already done so, complete the exercises in Chapter 14, particular the first one. You need to have questions and their corresponding answers to practice with. So gather your questions, answer them on paper first, then start practicing them by yourself.

2. Now, sit in front of a mirror and answer the questions so that you can see your facial expressions and body language while you are answering them. Watch out for improper posture, overuse of hand gestures, unconscious body language, and so forth.

3. Find a friend or family member, and do a little role-playing. I know this seems silly now, but you won't think it's silly when you confidently walk into an interview and knock the ball out of the park, so to speak. This is the closest you can get to the real thing and is the absolute best way to prepare. Don't just practice answering questions; also work on your greeting and departure. Every part of the interview, even when you are not speaking, says something about you. If you have a video camera (even a smartphone will do), record the mock interviews.

4. After your mock interviews, ask the practice interviewer and any observers for their feedback. Ask them to be completely honest. It does you no good if they are just going to stroke

your ego to be nice. Make a list of their suggestions so you know what to work on. Also review the video recording so you can observe yourself. Do you agree with the feedback of your mock interviewer(s)? Did you identify anything they didn’t mention?

16 DRESS FOR SUCCESS

When it comes to job interviews, one of the biggest mistakes that job seekers can make involves their appearance, namely the clothing that they choose to wear. The three main rules of interviewing are professionalism, professionalism, and professionalism! This cannot be said enough. Your appearance says a lot about you, your level of commitment, and your professionalism. The worst mistake you can make is showing up for a job interview like you were simply taking a trip to the mall. Not carefully planning your appearance, especially your clothes, can quickly eliminate you as a candidate for job.

If you are a well-seasoned career professional, this may sound trivial to you. If so, feel free to either continue reading or skip ahead to the next chapter. If you are new to the workforce or are transitioning to a new level in your career, I would advise you to keep reading.

Now, when you are heading into an interview, wearing professional clothing, such as a dress or suit, shows that you are serious about the job and making a good impression. Your professionalism and responsibility will be brought to light as well. You may be surprised to know that many job interviewers remember the appearance of their applicants before all else. One person I once interviewed with commented that she was impressed by the fact that I was wearing a belt. This was for a six-figure job, and it seemed so obvious. When I expressed curiosity by her comment, she said, "You would be surprised by what some people actually wear to an interview. Attention to the little things is a big deal to me."

If you are serious about finding a job or landing the job of your dreams, go the extra mile—put your best foot forward. With that in mind, different individuals have different definitions of professionalism. When trying to determine what you should wear to a job interview, you have a number of factors to consider. For instance, it is advised that men wear suits, including a pressed button-down dress shirt and tie. Women should wear a skirt suit or dress slacks and blouse. Always limit jewelry, and if you have piercings other than in your ears, it is recommended that you remove them for the interview.

While this is the general rule, there may be extenuating circumstances where formal attire is not appropriate. Just use your best judgment and always err on the side of caution. It is better to be overdressed than underdressed. If you have done your research and are familiar with the industry, company, and individual with whom you will be meeting, you should have a good idea of what is acceptable and what is not.

In addition to dressing professionally for a job interview, you may want to consider doing the same for your submission process. If you will be submitting your job applications or resumes in person, dress as you would for a job interview. You never know when you may get the opportunity to quickly meet with the supervisor who will be handling all job interviews. This is your best opportunity to make a good first impression. It is also important to mention that in some businesses, such as retail for instance, supervisors often choose to give job interviews right on the spot. That is why you will want to dress as if you were attending a job interview, even when just submitting your job applications and resumes.

Although you may have a suitable outfit in your closet already, you may want to consider going shopping. If for no other reason, this can be a good sanity check to ensure that what you own is not terribly outdated. If it is, and it is possible for you to do so, make the investment in a nice, tailored, professional-looking outfit. In fact, you may also want to consider making an appointment at your local barbershop or hair salon to at least clean up around the edges. Anything you can do to look your best can give you an edge. You may be surprised, but these simple steps can also be a confidence booster. This confidence can help you successfully breeze through your next job interview.

Chapter 16 Exercises

Chapter 16 was a short but important one. It's sad, but I've seen many people go through the tedious process of writing a killer resume and cover letter, and spend enormous amounts of time and money finding job leads and landing interviews, only to negate all this hard work within the first thirty seconds of the interview. The problem? They neglected basic hygiene or professional dress standards. Don't let this happen to you! This is so easy. With all the other things job seekers have to contend with along the way, it's silly to create your own obstacles. These exercises are simple and self-explanatory. I'm sure you already have this covered, but humor me! If nothing else, it's a good sanity check.

1. Make sure you have current, fresh-looking attire available. For guys, this means a suit, including a professional tie. For ladies, this could be a pant or skirt suit or a professional dress. Whatever outfit you choose, it should be modest and professional; nothing revealing. You want the interviewer to be focused on the dialogue, not distracted by anything below the neck. If you don't have anything current, buy something. You don't want something outdated or worn looking. Either way, make sure you have the clothing professionally cleaned and pressed.

2. Clean up. Shower, get a haircut, and make sure it is properly brushed and styled. Trim your nails and make sure there's no dirt under them. For guys, facial hair can be tricky. Some managers demand none at all—clean shaven. Others are more lenient, but you may not know this in advance. If you are going to keep a moustache or beard, just make sure it is short and has crisp trim lines.

3. Don't forget about the accessories. Polish your shoes and wear a belt if applicable. A little modest jewelry is okay, but don't go in looking like Mr. T with big gaudy chains hanging down your chest. Also, I would recommend losing any piercings, except for a nice set of earrings for ladies, during the interview. Sorry, gentlemen, but some people are still very conservative, so I'd lose the earrings just to be safe.

   Regardless of gender, remove any other piercings (nose, tongue, eyebrow, etc.) that could be visible for the interview. Finally, if you have any large tattoos, try to cover them as best you can during the interview. I'm not casting judgment on anyone's choice of body art, be it ink or bling, but some people judge books by their covers; namely, many interviewers. You might resist it, but this is a simple step you can take to help land that job.

17 HANDLING SPONTANEOUS INTERVIEWS

By now, you understand the importance of preparing for the big job interview, right? But sometimes the most carefully laid plans do not work out exactly how we wanted. There may be times when you decide to walk in to a company to submit a job application or your resume. Many professionals recommend submitting job applications and resumes in person whenever possible.

Job fairs are also valuable events that allow you to meet with potential employers in person and apply for job openings. In many, if not most instances, you will have your resume accepted and you will be told that you will be contacted for a job interview in the future. However, you just might receive a spontaneous job interview. If and when that time comes, do you know what you should do?

Before we answer that question, it is first important that we define our terms. Essentially, spontaneous job interviews are those that are impromptu or without much notice, and they come in a number of different formats. For instance, a manager may contact you and ask you to come in for a job interview that day or the following day. Although you are given some notice, many are unable to prepare as much as they would have liked for an interview that is scheduled right away. You may also find yourself having a job interview right on the spot. This is not uncommon, especially in the retail and food service industries.

As nice as it is to have immediate response to your application, these interviews can be scary and overwhelming for many. With that in mind, you should know that there are both a number of advantages and disadvantages to this type of job interview. One of those benefits is the need it shows. If employers are looking to interview you right on the spot, or if they are looking to set up a job interview as soon as possible, there is a good chance that they need to hire an employee right away. This vital need can significantly increase your chances of not only getting the job, but also leveraging the opportunity to negotiate compensation in your favor. At the same time, spontaneous or last-minute job interviews do not give you much time for preparation. Without preparation, it can be hard to perform up to your standards.

Although spontaneous or last-minute job interviews do make preparation difficult, there are a number of steps that you can take to be ready for them, just in case. For starters, we already discussed the importance of dressing appropriately. Make sure you have a professional-looking, tailored, and pressed outfit ready at all times. Even if you are just submitting your job application or your resume, make sure your appearance is professional. A manager who decides to offer you a job interview right away should expect you to be somewhat unprepared, but why not take a few extra steps, like putting on a nice outfit, to show that you can be prepared for just about anything.

Some job seekers prefer spontaneous interviews, while others fear them. This fear is usually due to a sense of unpreparedness. Don't be afraid; be prepared! This preparation may involve conducting a mock interview with your friends or family members, using the Internet to research common job interview questions, researching the company you are applying to, and so forth.

Taking a few minutes or a few hours, at the most, to prepare for a job interview, even if one has yet to be scheduled, will do no harm. In fact, it is likely that you would take these approaches later on, so why not get a head start? In a nutshell, be proactive about the preparation tips we have already discussed and expect the unexpected.

As nerve-wracking as last-minute or spontaneous job interviews can be, you should refrain from turning any down, as they can literally be the opportunity of a lifetime. As long as you have been proactive in your preparation, spontaneous job interviews should not be that scary. In fact, if you have been following all the steps in this book so far, you should be expecting lots of calls, and you should be ready for them!

What about spontaneous phone interviews? Someone once told me a story about receiving a call on a Sunday and having an impromptu interview that went horribly wrong. Her lesson: "I've since learned I should have asked to schedule it a day or two later, which would have given me time to prepare and would have made me look more professional—like I knew what I was doing." This is great advice! Do everything you can to be on your toes, but if possible, request to schedule a formal date and time to allow you to prepare.

18 WHAT *NOT* TO DO ON INTERVIEWS

We have spent time in previous chapters talking about things that you should do and discuss during a job interview. However, sometimes what is *not* said is just as important as what *is* said. Simply put, there are some topics that need to be discussed during a job interview, and there are others that should be left out of the conversation.

One of the many topics that you should refrain from discussing at one of your upcoming job interviews involves your personal life. For instance, unless explicitly asked, keep your friends and family out of the discussion. If you are asked personal questions, assuming they are not too personal or offensive, you should respond honestly, but it is usually best to refrain from bringing up the topic yourself. As much as possible, try to keep your personal and professional lives separate.

You must also refrain from divulging important information about your past employer. If the previous employer is a competitor of the company you are currently interviewing with, you may be in violation of a noncompete or nondisclosure agreement, which could have legal ramifications. Simply taking the high road and avoiding any topics that involve poor experiences at your previous places of employment should help your public perception. You never have the need to be concerned when you do the right thing!

A bad experience at a previous job is another topic to avoid. For starters, sharing this kind of information may be deemed as gossiping, complaining, or making excuses for something. Best case, this is a credibility killer.

Similarly, never speak poorly about any of your former supervisors. Regardless of whether your boss was in the wrong, refrain from speaking about the conflict. That does not mean that you should lie if asked, but it does mean that you should use your best judgment and restrain yourself. You want to show all prospective employers that you have respect for management, even if you do not like the management members.

If you were ever terminated from a job, proceed with caution during your job interviews. Discussing a job from which you were terminated generally will not work in your best interest, although the nature of the termination is a factor. For instance, you should avoid discussing any serious infringements, such as sexual harassment or theft, during a job interview. Again, do not lie if asked; just do not offer the information. However, if you will receive a background check, this information may come to light anyway. If you were released from a job because of no fault of your own, such as a downsizing, this is typically not as damaging, but still use caution when discussing it.

Compensation is another topic best avoided during an initial interview. This may sound counterintuitive to some, as a job interview is the place to ask questions in general, but compensation is unique. Some experts may disagree with this, but I have a lot of practical, real-world experience that has taught me that bringing up the topic of salary and benefits too early can impose uncomfortable pressure on both parties during the entire hiring process. It may also give the interviewer the impression that all you are interested in is money.

The purpose of the job interview is for both parties to get to know each other and determine if there is a mutual fit. If there is a fit, the topic of compensation will eventually come up anyway and can be addressed during negotiations. (Stay tuned for more information on negotiations.) If either or both parties decide you may not be the best candidate for the position, then discussions of pay are of no consequence.

Often, an interviewer will bring up salary. This may be a trap to get you back on your heels and give him or her the upper hand, which they can use in later negotiations. If an interviewer asks what your current or previous salary was, answer honestly and try to move past the topic. If he or she comes right out and ask you how much money you want, simply ask, “Wow, should I construe this as a job offer?” Most often, interviewers will say no and that they were just curious. If this happens, just politely tell them, “With all due respect, I feel it may be a little early to discuss compensation, and I generally like to reserve that topic until we’ve determined that there is a mutual fit.”

This may seem pretty bold, but again, I have done this on more than one occasion, and I have yet to have anyone who did not respect this answer.

There are a number of other “taboo” topics that should be avoided during an interview, including sex, religion, and politics. These, as well as those previously discussed, are just a few areas of conversation that can doom an interview and your chances of landing the job. Of course, it is important to answer all questions asked, but just be cautious with your answers and do not divulge more information than needed.

Step 5
Negotiating

Earn What You Are Worth!

19 NEGOTIATING YOUR COMPENSATION

Okay, so Step 5 is only one chapter, but it could be the most important in this book. In my opinion, this is what it is all about, and for me, it is the most fun of the entire job search process. It can be exhilarating to gain the most leverage possible and use that leverage to secure a handsome payoff.

All the work you have done to get to this point, as outlined in the previous chapters, is for naught if you ultimately do not end up with a compensation package that you will be satisfied with. Money is the most sensitive issue in the whole hiring process. Discussing compensation often causes anxiety for both employee and employer. Here are eight ways to make the process of salary negotiations efficient.

1. Do your research. Before the interview process begins, it is best to have a basic idea of what the compensation range is for the type of position you are applying for relative to the industry, specifically in your geographic area. You can generally find this information on various career websites, such as Monster.com and others. You can also contact a local professional organization that represents your career field. Additional salary range information is available at American Almanac of Jobs and Salaries, National Association of Colleges and Employers, Career Center, and professionals in your related field.

   As soon as you have a general idea of the salary and benefit expectations, you can now examine your monthly cash requirements. Remember that when taxes are figured into the mix, approximately 30 percent of your gross monthly salary is deducted, possibly more, depending on your benefits and other deductions. Hopefully you have done some research before you are too heavily invested in a particular career path. You do not want to spend a lot of time, money, and effort pursuing a career that cannot realistically support your desired lifestyle.

2. Determine your skills. You should understand that different segments of the economy require a variety of skills depending on the industry setting. Once you have established what your skills are and what they are worth to the current employment market, you should know the limitations of your negotiation.

3. Weigh the company's compensation package. To determine your fair market value for a specific job, consider the economic, geographic, and industry factors of the job offer. Aside from salary, consider the value of fringe benefits, including promotions, medical insurance, paid time off, tuition assistance, career-specific training, and retirement plans (e.g., 401(k), pension) to ensure a fair proposed compensation package.

No matter what, it is important to know what your bottom line is before entering any negotiation. When going into the negotiation, I always know the minimum I am willing to accept, what I would like to have, and a stretch goal. This applies not just to salary but also to benefits; the total package. Be prepared to walk if the employer is unwilling to negotiate an offer that at least meets your minimum threshold.

4. Sell your value. If you know that what you could offer the company justifies a larger income, stay humble, but do not back down. Once you sell yourself discreetly, and later more directly, an honest and fair interviewer should understand whether the company's salary proposal is appropriate.

   Remember, some interviewers will ask you about your salary history to paint you into a corner during negotiations. Always tell the truth when it comes to your past salary, but avoid basing your desired salary on your current salary. You deserve to be paid what is commensurate with the industry and based on the value you can bring to the organization. Taking a tip from Brian Tracy, I once said this to a potential employer who pushed back on my salary demands due to my previous salary:

I understand where you are coming from; however, I feel that comparing my previous position with this one is like comparing apples and oranges. Based on my experience and the tremendous value we both believe I can add to your company, I believe that my salary request is fair, wouldn't you agree?

You may not get everything you want, but believe me, this is a killer line and will be a feather in your cap throughout the negotiations. Use it!

5. Remain patient. No matter what you do, *never* accept (nor reject, for that matter) the employer's initial offer on the spot. Doing so leaves no room for negotiation. Whenever a potential employer makes me an offer, I say:

    I appreciate your offer, but this is an important decision for my family and me, so I would like forty-eight hours to mull this over and give it full consideration.

I do this every time I am negotiating a job offer, and it works like a charm. This is so powerful, as it shows the employer your poise and professionalism and that you are not desperate (even if you are). Do not be afraid that the employer will withdraw his or her offer if you do this. I have never had that happen. Most people respect your desire to do things "right." If this is not acceptable to them, move on. You do not want to work there anyway!

Making employers wait a couple of days will often make them anxious and pliable in their negotiations. It is like playing hard to get. What is it about human nature that seems to make us want something we may not be able to have? I have heard of others who have used this technique, only to have the hiring manager call them back inside of the forty-eight hours to say that he or she really wanted them on the team and ask what it was going to take for them to move forward. If this happens, you are in the exact position you want to be in. If not, read on to find out how you should proceed.

First and foremost, always call the employer

back when you promised you would. If you told him or her forty-eight hours, then do not make them wait forty-nine. On the other hand, if you have made your decision prior to the forty-eight hours, do not call back too soon. A couple of hours before the deadline is about the earliest you want to call back to avoid coming across as desperate.

When you do call the employer back, or preferably meet in person, remain calm and say something like this:

Good morning, Mr./Mrs. Johnson, this is <insert your name>. As promised, I have spent the last couple days carefully considering your offer, and this is the conclusion I have come to. While I appreciate the offer, based on my skills and experience, and the value I can bring to ABC Company, I believe a salary of $xx,xxx would be fair for this position.

Notice two powerful negotiation tips here. Do not end the sentence with the dollar amount, as this will resonate in the other person's mind and will become his or her whole focus. Instead, place the amount in the middle of the sentence before you use the word *fair*. Yes, use the word *fair*, as no one wants to be perceived as unfair; you are planting a subconscious seed in the person's mind.

Once you have finished this sentence, go completely silent. That's right, do not say another word! This is another tried-and-true sales technique, and it is the only time during the entire negotiation process where it is okay to induce an uncomfortable situation. Whoever speaks first loses.

You threw down the gauntlet; now the pressure is on the other person to respond. The person's response will determine how you proceed and what you say. The worst he or she can say is no, and if that happens, you can still negotiate other terms if the salary is acceptable.

6. Be fair and realistic. In negotiating, never compete. Negotiation is basically a process that should benefit both parties. Understand your needs and those of the company. If the negotiation does not result in a win-win situation (i.e., both

parties are satisfied with the results), then ultimately it is not a deal worth doing.

7. Never give something for nothing. This is an age-old technique that applies to any situation where you are negotiating, not just compensation. As we have discussed, negotiating is a process of give and get. For example, if the prospective employer wants to throw conditions into the agreement, such as requiring overtime or travel, then you should counter with some terms by which his or her demands are acceptable to you. This could come in the form of a higher salary, additional paid time off, or another benefit. The bottom line is, you should always get something of equal value in return for giving something in the negotiation. Never concede the upper hand.

8. Know when the offer is final. Be aware when the negotiation is done. In other words, do not oversell it. Pushing further when a deal has been set could give a negative first impression on your part. You do not want to be viewed as greedy, or one who is prone to go back on his or her word. Again, if *both*

parties are not satisfied with the outcome of the negotiation, this could result in an awkward relationship with some deep-seated bitterness. All that being said, if the employer comes back to you with proposed changes after an agreement has already been reached, then all bets are off. You are then free to negotiate as you previously did.

Based on a survey conducted by the Society for Human Resource Management, four out of five employers are willing to negotiate compensation. Understanding the tips outlined in this chapter will allow you to enhance the terms of your new job. Just remember to stay professional throughout the entire process. Also, remember that you may not be able to come to terms with every potential employer you negotiate with. That is okay. Just like in sales, you are not going to win every deal. It is up to you to keep moving forward until you find the situation that is the best fit for you.

Chapter 19 Exercises

What are you worth? This was really the point of Chapter 19—asking for what you are worth! Negotiating a compensation package can be nerve-wracking, but this has grown to become my favorite part of the process. It is your one opportunity to take advantage of the leverage you have. Once you are hired, you will likely never have this same bargaining power again, so make it count!

1. Before you can negotiate, you need to know what you are negotiating for. Use the Internet, specifically some of the job search websites, to conduct a little research. Find out what the going salaries and benefits are for your chosen

career field. Many resources break this down by region, as salaries often vary depending on where you live. For instance, salaries in Los Angeles are generally higher than those in St. Louis. This is due to competition and, quite frankly, the availability of funds in different parts of the country. So, find the going compensation rates in your part of the country.

2. Now, what do you realistically think you are worth? Write down your target salary, the absolute minimum you are willing to accept, and a stretch goal (silly money over your target goal). You will start your negotiations at your stretch goal, and employers will often make an offer around your minimum. You are often left somewhere in the middle, hopefully at or above your target salary.

3. Besides salary, what else do you want and need to be part of the compensation package? Vacation time, health insurance, retirement plan, and continuing education are all common in most professional settings. Again, determine what the "must-haves" are versus the "nice-to-

haves." Often, you can give a little in salary for better benefits and vice versa. It's all about what's important to you.

4. Work on your counteroffer "pitch." Remember, never accept an offer on the spot. Request twenty-four to forty-eight hours to think it over and call them back. This puts you in a position of control, but you have to be able to deliver, so know what you are going to say when you call back. Never negotiate on an ad-hoc basis. This makes you look like a pushover, and you will likely lose the negotiations.

5. Before going into a negotiation, reread Chapter 19 very carefully and review your answers to these exercises.

WRAPPING IT ALL UP

As I hope I have demonstrated in this book, the job search process does not have to be overwhelming. To use an old cliché, how do you eat an elephant? One bite at a time! So it is with finding a job. You just have to break the process down into manageable steps. This approach will allow you to better organize and prepare yourself, to reduce the stress involved. Let's review:

Planning. Setting out a plan is the key to getting off to a good start. It lays the foundation for the rest of the job search process, as success is much more likely if you have a plan. You need to reconcile where you are currently, where you want to be, and how you are going to get there. In fact, this is about more than just finding a job; it is about setting a course for your career. You deserve all the happiness that life has to offer, but it is up to you to define happiness for yourself and *carpe diem*—seize the day!

Preparing. You may have created a plan and have your career blueprint, but do you have the tools to build it? Quite simply, you need to have a well-written cover letter and resume, including solid references. Most employers for advanced, professional-level positions will not even talk to you until they have seen these items. Hopefully you have leveraged the tips in Step 2 to make the development of these tools easier.

Searching. There are so many resources available today to help you find a job. From the classics, like the employment section of the newspaper classified ads, to the latest in Internet technology, there is no excuse for not getting out there and "just doing it." Plus, do not forget to leverage friends, family, and other contacts; word-of-mouth is still the best form of advertising! There is no reason to limit yourself. Use all the tools available to increase your chances. To return to our fishing analogy, the more lines you cast, the better your chances of getting a bite.

Interviewing. Ah, yes, the interview. This is your time to shine. This is where all your experience, training, and preparation come together and allow you to sell yourself as "the one." Equally important, though, this is your chance to interview the employer. You get to ask questions and determine if this company is the right one for you. You spend so much time preparing and searching for the right opportunity, but more important, you have to spend at least eight hours a day, five days a week on the job, so you had better make sure this is a job you think you will enjoy and help you achieve your career goals.

Negotiating. Let's face it, most of us work simply as the means by which we pay the bills, support our lifestyles, and prepare for long-term financial security. While money is not the only consideration, you would be hard pressed to convince me that it is not at least one of the most important. You have the most negotiating leverage before you accept the job offer, so get it right before you say yes. Once you are on the job, the employer has the upper hand. Know what you want before going into it, and hold firm. Just keep your cool and be fair.

Well, we have come a long way and have covered quite a bit of material. While each topic has not been covered in exhaustive detail, I have provided you with the most important information in an efficient and practical manner. I believe this to be more effective and usable than trying to overwhelm you with needless reading. What is important is that you have the necessary weapons in your arsenal. If you carefully study and put this material into action, I know it will help you as it has helped me over the years.

Good luck and God bless!

USEFUL RESOURCES FOR JOB SEEKERS

Professional Development Websites

www.mycareerfasttrack.com

www.briantracy.com

www.tonyrobbins.com

Popular Job Search Websites

www.monster.com

www.careerbuilder.com

www.theladders.com

Essential Social Networking Websites

www.facebook.com

www.twitter.com

www.linkedin.com

Career-Related Books

Are You Sabotaging Your Own Career? by Brandon Grieve

The Pathfinder by Nicholas Lore

Guerilla Marketing for Job Hunters 2.0 by Jay Conrad Levinson

Really Good Authors (Read anything by them!):

Brian Tracy

Tony Robbins

Zig Ziglar

ABOUT THE AUTHOR

Brandon Grieve is an author, speaker, trainer, and

entrepreneur based in the St. Louis, MO, area. In addition to writing *How To Get On The Career Fast Track,* he has written and published the e-book *Are You Sabotaging Your Own Career?,* where he outlines common ways individuals cause their own career roadblocks and how to overcome them. Prior to founding Career Fast Track, LLC, Brandon spent several years building a successful information technology career. He now leverages his professional experiences in the pursuit of his mission to help individuals find happiness and purpose in their careers. For more information on Brandon Grieve or Career Fast Track, LLC, please visit:

Web: www.mycareerfasttrack.com

Facebook: www.facebook.com/careerfasttrack

Twitter: twitter.com/mycareerfast

www.ingramcontent.com/pod-product-compliance
Lightning Source LLC
Chambersburg PA
CBHW031544040426
42452CB00006B/171

* 9 7 8 0 9 8 5 8 3 0 5 0 2 *